Quick and Easy, P  es

Cookies & Bakes

Publisher's Note: Raw or semi-cooked eggs should not be consumed by babies, toddlers, pregnant or breastfeeding women, the elderly or those suffering from a chronic illness.

Publisher & Creative Director: Nick Wells
Senior Project Editor: Catherine Taylor
Art Director: Mike Spender
Layout Design: Jane Ashley
Digital Design & Production: Chris Herbert

Special thanks to Esme Chapman, Emma Chafer and Frances Bodiam.

This is a **FLAME TREE** Book

FLAME TREE PUBLISHING
Crabtree Hall, Crabtree Lane
Fulham, London SW6 6TY
United Kingdom
www.flametreepublishing.com

First published 2013

ISBN: 978-0-85775-810-1

A copy of the CIP data for this book is available from the British Library.

Printed in Singapore

All pictures © Flame Tree Publishing Ltd except the following, which are courtesy Shutterstock.com and the following photographers:
9b Poulsons Photography; 10t Marie C Fields; 20 nastiakru; 24b IngridHS.

Quick and Easy, Proven Recipes

Cookies & Bakes

**FLAME TREE
PUBLISHING**

Contents

Essentials

Everyone loves a home bake: from the irresistible smells wafting from the kitchen, to the rustic, homely presentation, nothing beats 'em. This invaluable little book is stuffed full of easy recipes for moreish cookies and sweet treats, but first remind yourself of the kitchen and baking essentials, including equipment, ingredients, hygiene and techniques, and even how to handle chocolate.

Introduction

č

The sheer range of cookies and bakes in the world is amazing! This book will not only show you how to make some of them, but will also save you money – shop-bought fare is quite expensive, so you will definitely notice the difference in price. Also, there is really no comparison to the quality of home-made treats and the fun to be had in making and baking them. A batch of home-made cookies also brings a personal touch to any celebration. Baking is also a good way to introduce children to the art of cookery and these recipes will help to teach the basic techniques. On top of all this, baking gives so much pleasure: you get a real sense of satisfaction when you create a fresh batch of delicious bakes. So choose a recipe that appeals, get out your mixing bowls and start baking!

How to Use This Book

If you are a first-time or less experienced baker, remember that there are no secrets to baking – just follow our simple step-by-step guides to ensure successful results. The choice is yours – you can make chocolate chip cookies or ginger snaps, lemon bars or flapjacks.

Everybody loves home bakes, and friends always welcome old favourites, but everyone loves to try new treats. The first section in this book covers classic cookies and biscuits, including family favourites such as oatmeal raisin cookies or Italian biscotti to go with your coffee. There is also a great selection of bars and traybakes, from brownies to flapjacks, and a section with tasty cupcakes, buns and muffins.

Baking involves many different techniques and a little bit of skill is certainly needed for some of the bakes in this book, but you will be able to build up your confidence through practice. To help you achieve success every time, there are tips on choosing the right type of baking trays and paper liners. Using the very best ingredients is important, as are utensils and careful weighing and measuring. You will not achieve good results without first checking your oven for correct temperatures and exact timings (see below).

All methods and techniques are clearly explained, with colour photographs showing the finished result to aim for.

Check Your Oven

Each recipe begins with an oven setting, and it is important to preheat the oven to the correct temperature before placing the items in to bake. As well as preheating the oven, it is important to arrange the shelves in the correct position in the oven before you start. The best baking position is just above the centre of the oven and best results are achieved by baking only one batch at a time. If you bake two at once, you may find the lower one will come out not fully risen. Many of us have fan-assisted ovens. These circulate hot air round the oven and heat up very quickly. For fan ovens, you will need to reduce the temperature stated in the recipe by 10 per cent, which is usually 20°C. For example, if the stated temperature in a recipe is 180°C, reduce it to 160°C for a fan-assisted oven. However, ovens do vary, so follow your manufacturer's instructions and get

Introduction

to know the way your oven heats. If your oven is too hot, the outsides of the cookies or cakes will burn before the interior has had time to cook. If it is too cool, they may sink, not rise evenly or not crisp up appropriately. Try not to open the oven door until at least halfway through the baking time, when the items have had time to rise and set, if necessary, as a sudden drop in temperature will stop cake-like mixtures rising and they may sink.

Weighing and Measuring

All of the recipes in this book give metric and imperial measurements, but you must stick to one set only – i.e. only ever use either metric or imperial in one recipe – as they are not exact equivalents.

All spoon measurements should be used level (as opposed to 'heaped') for accuracy, and always use a recognised set of metric or imperial spoon measures for best results. Do not use domestic teaspoons and tablespoons as measures, as these may be deeper or shallower than a proper measuring spoon. Never estimate weights, as you will not achieve an accurate result.

Ingredients for baking should be weighed exactly and good kitchen scales are a vital piece of equipment for a baker. Old-fashioned scales with a pan and a set of weights, or modern ones with a digital display screen are equally good, as long as they are accurate. A measuring jug is vital for liquids and it needs to be marked with small measures for smaller amounts.

Equipment Needed

℮

Nowadays, you can get lost in the cookware sections of some of the larger stores – they really are a cook's paradise, with gadgets, cooking tools and state-of-the-art electronic blenders, mixers and liquidisers. A few well-picked, high-quality utensils and pieces of equipment will be frequently used and will therefore be a much wiser buy than cheaper gadgets.

Cooking equipment not only assists in the kitchen, but can make all the difference between success and failure. Take the humble tin: although a very basic piece of cooking equipment, it plays an essential role in baking. Using the incorrect size, for example, a tin that is too large, will spread the mixture too thinly and the result will be a flat, limp-looking bake. On the other hand, cramming the mixture into a tin which is too small will result in the mixture rising up and out of the tin.

Baking Trays & Tins

To ensure successful baking, it is worth investing in a selection of high-quality trays and tins, which, if looked after properly, should last for many years. Follow the manufacturers' instructions when first using and ensure that the tins are thoroughly washed and dried after use and before putting away.

Good baking sheets/trays are a must for baking cookies and biscuits. They may have very shallow raised sides, or be flat with just one raised side. Swiss roll tins are slightly deeper, with sides all around, and these can also be used for cookies or for shallow traybakes (such as 33 x 23 cm/ 13 x 9 inch).

Deeper, square or oblong baking tins are needed for making traybakes, brownies, flapjacks and so on. Some good sizes to buy are 18 cm/7 inch and 20.5 cm/8 inch square tins.

Then there are patty/bun trays, ideal for making small buns, jam tarts, fairy cakes or mince pies; larger muffin tins for classic deep cupcakes and muffins; and even individual Yorkshire pudding tins and muffin tins or flan tins.

If you get tempted to expand your baking repertoire into larger cakes, perhaps the most useful of tins are sandwich cake tins, ideal for classics such as Victoria sponge. You will need two tins (normally 18 cm/7 inches or 20.5 cm/8 inches in diameter and about 5–7.5 cm/2–3 inches deep).

Loaf tins are used for bread, fruit or tea bread and terrines, and normally come in two sizes, 450 g/1 lb and 900 g/2 lb. There are plenty of other tins to choose from, ranging from themed tins, such as Christmas trees, numbers from 1–9, as well as tins shaped as petals, ring mould tins (tins with a hole in the centre) and spring-form tins, where the sides release after cooking, allowing the finished cake to be removed easily.

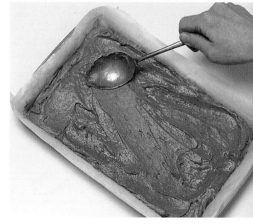

A selection of different-sized roasting tins are also a worthwhile investment, as they can double up as a bain marie, or for cooking larger quantities of cakes such as gingerbread. A few different tins and dishes are required if baking crumbles, soufflés and pies. Ramekin dishes and small pudding basins can be used for a variety of different recipes, as can small tartlet tins and dariole moulds.

Equipment Needed

Electrical Equipment

Nowadays, help from time-saving gadgets and electrical equipment makes baking far easier and quicker. Equipment can be used for creaming, mixing, beating, whisking, kneading, grating and chopping. There is a wide choice of machines available, from the most basic to the very sophisticated.

∿ Food Processors – First, decide what you need your processor to do when choosing a machine. If you are a novice to baking, it may be a waste to start with a machine which offers a wide range of implements and functions. This can be off-putting and result in not using the machine to its ultimate.

In general, while styling and product design play a role in the price, the more you pay, the larger the machine will be, with a bigger bowl capacity and many more gadgets attached. Nowadays, you can chop, shred, slice, chip, blend, purée, knead, whisk and cream anything. However, just what basic features should you ensure your machine has before buying it?

When buying a food processor, look for measurements on the side of the processor bowl and machines with a removable feed tube which allows food or liquid to be added while the motor is running. Look out for machines that have the facility to increase the capacity of the bowl (ideal when making soup) and have a pulse button for controlled chopping.

For many people, storage is an issue, so reversible discs and flex storage, or, on more advanced models, a blade storage compartment or box, can be a real advantage.

It is also worth thinking about machines which offer optional extras, which can be bought as your cooking requirements change. Mini-chopping bowls are available for those wanting to chop small quantities of food. If time is an issue, dishwasher-friendly attachments may be vital. Citrus presses, liquidisers and whisks may all be useful attachments for the individual cook.

❧ Blenders – Blenders often come as attachments to food processors and are generally used for liquidising and puréeing foods. There are two main types of blender. The first is known as a goblet blender. The blades of this blender are at the bottom of the goblet, with measurements up the sides. The second blender is portable. It is hand-held and should be placed in a bowl to blend.

❧ Food Mixers – These are ideally suited to mixing cakes and kneading dough, either as a table-top mixer or a hand-held mixer. Both are extremely useful and based on the same principle of mixing or whisking in an open bowl to allow more air to get to the mixture and therefore give a lighter texture.

The table-top mixers are freestanding and are capable of dealing with fairly large quantities of mixture. They are robust machines, capable of dealing easily with kneading dough and heavy cake mixing, as well as whipping cream,

❧   Equipment Needed

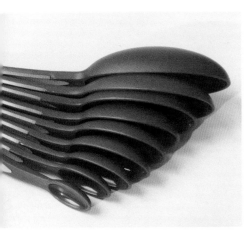

whisking egg whites or making one-stage cakes. These mixers also offer a wide range of attachments ranging from liquidisers, mincers, juicers, can openers and many more and varied attachments.

Hand-held mixers are smaller than freestanding mixers and often come with their own bowl and stand, from which they can be lifted off and used as hand-held devices. They have a motorised head with detachable twin whisks. These mixers are particularly versatile, as they do not need a specific bowl in which to whisk. Any suitable mixing bowl can be used.

Other Essential Equipment

- **Measuring Spoons** – A set of standard measuring spoons for accurate measuring of small quantities of ingredients is vital. Remember that all spoon measures should be level and do not use cutlery such as kitchen tablespoons or teaspoons, as these sizes differ and may be inaccurate.

- **Sieves** – Use a large, wire sieve for sifting flour and dry ingredients together and keep a smaller one, ideally nylon, aside just for icing sugars. Sieves help remove impurities and sift air into the flour, encouraging the mixture to be lighter in texture.

- **Mixing Bowls** – You will need a set of different-size mixing bowls (three to four sizes are useful) for beating small and large amounts of mixture, frostings and icings.

❧ Wooden Spoon – Keep an old-fashioned, large wooden spoon aside for baking, for beating butters and creaming. Do not use one that has been used for frying savoury things such as onions, as the flavours will taint the cake mixture.

❧ Rolling Pin – Essential for some biscuits, and for pastry. Ideally a rolling pin should be long and thin, heavy enough to roll dough out easily but not too heavy that it is uncomfortable to use. Pastry needs to be rolled out on a flat surface and although a lightly floured flat surface will do, a marble slab will ensure that the pastry is kept cool and that the fats do not melt while being rolled. This helps to keep the pastry light, crisp and flaky rather than heavy and stodgy, which happens if the fat melts before being baked.

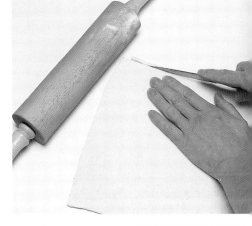

❧ Cookie Cutters – There are many different cutters available in metal or plastic, all suitable for cutting out the uncooked dough. Shapes range from animals, hearts and letters to fluted, round or square, in all sizes. Make sure the dough is of even thickness and you put the cutter squarely on the rolled dough for a uniform and even result.

❧ Cookie Cutters – You can also use a pastry wheel to cut out cookie shapes freeform; or for trimming pastry.

❧ Pastry Brush – A pastry brush is used for brushing glazes over cakes and melted butter round trays. As brushes tend to wear out regularly and shed their bristles, keep a spare new brush to hand.

- Kitchen Scissors – Scissors are essential for many small jobs, including cutting papers to size and snipping cherries, dried fruits or nuts into chunks.

- Grater – A grater is useful for grating citrus zests, chocolate and marzipan. Choose one with a fine and a coarse side.

- Spatula – For transferring mixture from the mixing bowl to the baking tins and spreading the mixture once it is in the tins.

- Palette Knife – To ease cakes and buns out of their tins before placing them on the wire racks to cool.

- Cake Tester or Skewer – Use a small, thin, metal skewer for inserting into the centre of a cake to test if it is ready. This is a handy piece of equipment but, if you do not have one, a clean, thin, metal knitting needle may be used instead.

- Wire Racks – Racks are vital to allow air to circulate round the hot cakes to let them cool down quickly, which prevents them from becoming moist or soggy underneath.

- Piping Bags and Nozzles – A nylon piping bag that comes with a set of five nozzles is a very useful piece of equipment for decorating cookies and sweet treats with icings. Look for a set with a plain nozzle and various star nozzles for piping swirls of buttercream.

The larger the star nozzle, the wider the swirls will be on the finished cakes.

Disposable paper or clear plastic icing bags are available, but nylon piping bags can be washed out in warm soapy water and dried out, ready to reuse again and again.

To Make a Paper Icing Bag

❧ Cut out a 38 x 25.5 cm/15 x 10 inch rectangle of greaseproof paper. Fold it diagonally in half to form two triangular shapes. Cut along the fold line to make two triangles. One of these triangles can be used another time – it is quicker and easier to make two at a time from one square than to measure and mark out a triangle on a sheet of paper.

❧ Fold one of the points on the long side of the triangle over the top to make a sharp cone and hold in the centre. Fold the other sharp end of the triangle over the cone.

❧ Hold all the points together at the back of the cone, keeping the pointed end sharp. Turn the points inside the top edge, fold over to make a crease, then secure with a piece of sticky tape.

❧ To use, snip away the end, place a piping nozzle in position and fill the bag with icing, or fill the bag with icing first, then snip away a tiny hole at the end for piping a plain edge, writing or piping tiny dots.

Equipment Needed

Essential Baking Ingredients

The quantities may differ, but basic baking ingredients do not vary greatly. Let us take a closer look at the baking ingredients which are essential.

Fat

Butter and firm block margarine are the fats most commonly used in baking. Others can also be used, such as white vegetable fat, lard and oil. Low-fat spreads are not recommended, as they tend to break down when they are cooked at a very high temperature. Often, it is simply a matter of personal preference which fat you decide to use when baking, but there are still a few guidelines that it is very important to remember.

Unsalted butter is the fat most commonly used in cake making, especially in rich fruit cakes and the heavier sponge cakes such as Madeira or chocolate torte. Unsalted butter gives a distinctive flavour to the cake. Some people favour margarine, which imparts little or no flavour to the cake.

As a rule, firm margarine and butter should not be used straight from the refrigerator but allowed to come to room temperature before using. Also, it should be beaten by itself first before creaming or rubbing in. Soft margarine is best suited to one-stage recipes. If oil is used, care should be taken – it is a good idea to follow a specific recipe, as the proportions of oil to flour and eggs are different. Fat is an integral ingredient when making pastry; again, there are a few specific guidelines to bear in mind.

For shortcrust pastry, the best results are achieved by using equal amounts of lard or white vegetable fat with butter or block margarine. The amount of fat used is always half the amount of flour.

Other pastries use differing amounts of ingredients. Pâté sucrée (a sweet flan pastry) uses all butter with eggs and a little sugar, while flaky or puff pastry uses a larger proportion of fat to flour and relies on the folding and rolling during making to ensure that the pastry rises and flakes well. When using a recipe, refer to the instructions to obtain the best result.

Flour

We can buy a wide range of flour, all designed for specific jobs. Strong flour, which is rich in gluten, whether it is white or brown (this includes granary and stoneground), is best kept for bread and Yorkshire pudding. It is also recommended for steamed suet puddings, as well as puff pastry. '00' flour is designed for pasta making and there is no substitute for this flour.

Essential Baking Ingredients

Ordinary flour or weak flour is best for cakes, biscuits and sauces, which absorb the fat easily and give a soft, light texture. This flour comes in plain white or self-raising, as well as wholemeal.

Self-raising flour, which has the raising agent already incorporated, is best kept for sponge cakes, where it is important that an even rise is achieved. Plain flour can be used for all types of baking and sauces. If using plain flour for scones or cakes and puddings, unless otherwise stated in the recipe, use 1 teaspoon of baking powder to 225 g/8 oz of plain flour.

With sponge cakes and light fruit cakes, it is best to use self-raising flour, as the raising agent has already been added to the flour. This way, there is no danger of using too much, which can result in a sunken cake with a sour taste.

There are other raising agents that are also used. Some cakes use bicarbonate of soda with or without cream of tartar, blended with warm or sour milk. Whisked eggs also act as a raising agent, as the air trapped in the egg ensures that the mixture rises. Generally, no other raising agent is required.

Some flour also comes ready-sifted which can be a benefit when using it for baking. There is even a special sponge flour designed especially for whisked sponges. Also, it is possible to buy flours that cater for coeliacs, which contain no gluten. Buckwheat, soya and chickpea flours are also available.

Eggs

When a recipe states '1 egg', it is generally accepted that this refers to a medium egg. Over the past few years, the grading of eggs has changed. For years, eggs were sold as small, standard and large, then this method changed and they were graded in numbers, with 1 being the largest. The general feeling by the public was that this system was misleading, so now we buy our eggs as small, medium and large.

Due to the slight risk of salmonella, all eggs are now sold date-stamped to ensure that the eggs are used in their prime. This applies even to farm eggs, which are no longer allowed to be sold straight from the farm. Look for the lion quality stamp (on 75 percent of all eggs sold), which guarantees that the eggs come from hens vaccinated against salmonella, have been laid in the UK and are produced to the highest food safety and standards. All of these eggs carry a best-before date.

There are many types of eggs sold and it really is a question of personal preference which ones are chosen. All offer the same nutritional benefits. The majority of eggs sold in this country are from caged hens. These are the cheapest eggs and the hens have been fed on a manufactured mixed diet. Eggs should be stored in their box in the refrigerator, and kept away from foods with strong smells.

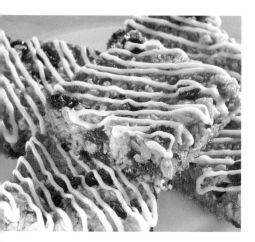

Barn eggs are from hens kept in barns who are free to roam within the barn. However, their diet is similar to caged hens and the barns may be overcrowded.

It is commonly thought that free-range eggs are from hens that lead a much more natural life and are fed natural foods. This, however, is not always the case and in some instances, they may still live in a crowded environment.

Four-grain eggs are from hens that have been fed on grain and no preventative medicines have been included in their diet. Organic eggs are from hens that live in a flock, whose beaks are not clipped and who are completely free to roam. Obviously, these eggs are much more expensive than the others.

Store eggs in the refrigerator with the round end uppermost (as packed in the egg boxes). Allow to come to room temperature before using. Do remember, raw or semi-cooked eggs should not be given to babies, toddlers, pregnant women, the elderly or those suffering from a recurring illness.

Sugar

Sugar not only offers taste to baking, but also adds texture and volume to the mixture. It is generally accepted that caster sugar is best for sponge cakes, puddings and meringues. Its fine granules disperse evenly when creaming or whisking. Granulated sugar is used for more general cooking, such as stewing fruit, whereas demerara sugar, with its toffee taste and crunchy texture, is good for sticky puddings and cakes such as flapjacks. For rich fruit cakes as well as Christmas puddings and cakes, use the muscovado sugars, which give a rich, intense molasses or treacle flavour.

Icing sugar is fine and powdery and is used primarily for icings. If used for icings it can be coloured using a few drops of food colouring or flavoured using citrus juice, cocoa powder or coffee extract. Icing sugar can also be used in meringues and in fruit sauces when the sugar needs to dissolve quickly. Always sift icing sugar at least once before use to remove lumps which would prevent a smooth texture from being achieved.

For a different taste, try flavouring your own sugar. Place a vanilla pod in a screw-top jar, fill with caster sugar, screw down the lid and leave for 2–3 weeks before using. Top up after use. Use thinly pared lemon or orange rind in the same manner.

If trying to reduce sugar intake, then use the unrefined varieties, such as golden granulated, golden caster, unrefined demerara and the muscovado sugars. All of these are a little sweeter than their refined counterparts, so less is required. Alternatively, clear honey or fructose (fruit sugar) can reduce sugar intake, as they have similar calories to sugar, but are twice as sweet. Also, they have a slow release, so their effect lasts longer. Dried fruits can also be included in the diet to top up sugar intake.

Essential Baking Ingredients

Essential Hygiene

℮

I t is well worth remembering that many foods can carry some form of bacteria. In most cases, the worst it will lead to is a bout of food poisoning or gastroenteritis, although for certain groups this can be more serious. The risk can be reduced or eliminated by good food hygiene and proper cooking.

Do not buy food that is past its sell-by date and do not consume any food that is past its use-by date. When buying food, use the eyes and nose to check if it is ok. If the food looks tired, limp or a bad colour or it has a rank, acrid or simply bad smell, do not buy or eat it under any circumstances.

Regularly clean, defrost and clear out the refrigerator and freezer – it is worth checking the packaging to see exactly how long each product is safe to freeze.

Dishcloths and tea towels must be washed and changed regularly. Ideally, use disposable cloths, which should be replaced on a daily basis. More durable cloths should be left to soak in bleach, then washed in the washing machine on a boil wash.

It is essential for hygiene in the kitchen that you always keep your hands, cooking utensils and food preparation surfaces clean and never allow pets to climb onto any work surfaces.

Buying

Avoid bulk buying where possible, especially fresh produce such as eggs, cream and fruit, unless buying for the freezer. Fresh foods lose their nutritional value rapidly, so buying a little at a time minimises loss of nutrients. It also eliminates a packed refrigerator, which reduces the effectiveness of the refrigeration process.

When buying frozen foods, ensure that they are not heavily iced on the outside. Place in the freezer as soon as possible after purchase.

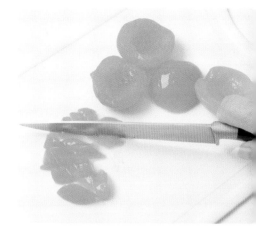

Preparation

Make sure that all work surfaces and utensils are clean and dry. Separate chopping boards should be used for raw and cooked ingredients. It is worth washing all fruits regardless of whether they are going to be eaten raw or lightly cooked.

Storing, Refrigerating and Freezing

All dairy products should be refrigerated. The temperature of the refrigerator should be between 1–5°C/34–41°F, while the freezer temperature should not rise above -18°C/-0.4°F. When refrigerating some cooked cakes,

allow them to cool down completely before refrigerating. Hot food will raise the temperature of the refrigerator and possibly affect or spoil other food stored in it.

Food within the refrigerator and freezer should always be covered. Raw ingredients should be placed on bottom shelves to avoid drips and cross-contamination.

Cookies and cakes are best stored in airtight cake tins. Biscuits and cookies should be layered with sheets of greaseproof paper or kitchen foil. If you use a plastic container rather than a tin, the goods may taste musty after a while and biscuits may go soggy.

High-risk Foods

Certain foods may carry risks to people who are considered vulnerable, such as the elderly, the ill, breastfeeding or pregnant women, babies and those suffering from a recurring illness. Such people are advised to treat the following foods with caution:

There is a slight chance that some eggs carry the bacteria salmonella. Therefore it is vital that you make sure that all eggs which are used in your baking are thoroughly cooked. Certain food items including mousses, soufflés and meringues all use raw or lightly cooked eggs, as do custard-based dishes, ice creams and sorbets.

Unpasteurised dairy products, especially soft cheese, all have the potential risk of listeria and should be avoided.

Basic Techniques

Creaming

Light cakes and buttery biscuits are made by the creaming method, which means that the butter and sugar are first beaten or 'creamed' together. A little care is needed for this method. Use a large mixing bowl to beat the fat and sugar together until pale and fluffy. The eggs are gradually beaten in to form a slackened batter and the flour is folded in last, to stiffen up the mixture. In some recipes, egg whites are whisked and added to the mixture separately for extra lightness. When the eggs are added, they are best used at room temperature to prevent the mixture from splitting or 'curdling'. Adding a teaspoon of flour with each beaten egg will help to keep the mixture light and smooth and prevent the mixture from separating. A badly mixed, curdled batter will hold less air and be heavy or can cause a sunken cake.

Preparing Tins

When recipes give instructions on how to prepare and line tins, these are important steps, so do not be tempted to skimp on these. The time and expense of baking cakes may be wasted if they will not turn out of the tin properly.

Rubbing In

In this method, the fat is lightly worked into the flour between the fingers, as in pastry making, until the mixture resembles fine crumbs. This can be done by hand or in a food processor. Enough liquid is stirred in to give a soft mixture that will drop easily from a spoon. This method is used for doughy cookies, easy fruit cakes and small buns such as rock cakes.

All-in-one Mixtures

This 'one-stage' method is quick and easy and is perfect for those new to baking, as it does not involve any complicated techniques. It is ideal for making light sponges, but soft tub-type margarine or softened butter at room temperature must be used. There is no need for any creaming or rubbing in, as all the ingredients are simply placed in a large bowl and quickly beaten together for just a few minutes until smooth. Be careful not to overbeat, as this will make the mixture too wet. Self-raising flour, with the addition of a little extra baking powder, is vital for a good rise.

The Melting Method

Cakes with a delicious moist, sticky texture, such as gingerbread, are made using this method. These cakes use a high proportion of sugar and syrup, which are gently warmed together in a saucepan with the fat, until the sugar granules have dissolved and the mixture is liquid. It is important to cool the hot melted mixture a little before beating in flour, eggs and spices to make a batter.

Basic Techniques

Handling Chocolate

Tips & Techniques

There are a few useful techniques for working with chocolate. None of them are very complicated, and all can be mastered easily with a little practice. These general guidelines apply equally for all types of chocolate,

Melting Chocolate

All types of chocolate are sensitive to temperature, so care needs to be taken during the melting process. It is also worth noting that different brands of chocolate have different consistencies when melting and when melted. Experiment with different brands to find one that you like.

As a general rule, it is important not to allow any water to come into contact with the chocolate. In fact, a drop or two of water is more dangerous than larger amounts, which may blend in. The melted chocolate will seize and it will be impossible to bring it back to a smooth consistency.

Do not overheat chocolate or melt it by itself in a pan over a direct heat. Always use either a double boiler or a heatproof bowl set over a saucepan of water, but do not allow the bottom of the bowl to come into contact with the water, as this will overheat the chocolate. Keep an eye on the chocolate, checking it every couple of minutes and reducing or extinguishing the heat under the saucepan as necessary. Stir the chocolate once or twice during melting until it is smooth and no lumps remain. Do not cover the bowl once the chocolate has melted or condensation will form, water will drop into it and it will be ruined. If the chocolate turns from a glossy, liquid mass into a dull, coarse, textured mess, you will have to start again.

Microwaving is another way of melting chocolate, but again, caution is required. Follow the oven manufacturer's instructions together with the instructions on the chocolate and proceed with care. Melt the chocolate in bursts of 30–60 seconds, stirring well between bursts, until the chocolate is smooth. If possible, stop microwaving before all the chocolate has melted and allow the residual heat in the chocolate to finish the job. The advantage of microwaving is that you do not need to use a saucepan, making the whole job quicker and neater.

Making Chocolate Decorations

❧ Curls and Caraque – Chocolate curls are made using a clean paint scraper. They are usually large, fully formed curls, which are useful for decorating gateaux and cakes. Caraque are long, thin curls, which can be used in the same way, but are less dramatic.

To make either shape, melt the chocolate following your preferred method and then spread it in a thin layer over a cool surface, such as a marble slab, ceramic tile or piece of

❧   Handling Chocolate

granite. Leave until just set but not hard. To make curls, take the clean paint scraper and set it at an angle to the surface of the chocolate, then push, taking a layer off the surface. This will curl until you release the pressure.

To make caraque, use a large, sharp knife and hold it at about a 45-degree angle to the chocolate. Hold the handle and the tip and scrape the knife towards you, pulling the handle but keeping the tip more or less in the same place. This method makes thinner, tighter, longer curls.

∾ Shaved Chocolate – Using a vegetable peeler, shave a thick block of chocolate to make minicurls. These are best achieved if the chocolate is a little soft, otherwise it has a tendency to break into little flakes.

∾ Chocolate Shapes – Spread a thin layer of chocolate, as described in the instructions for chocolate curls, and allow to set as before. Use shaped cutters or a sharp knife to cut out shapes. Use to decorate cakes.

∾ Chocolate Butterflies – Draw a butterfly shape on a piece of nonstick baking parchment. Fold the paper down the middle of the body of the butterfly to make a crease, then open the paper out flat. Pipe chocolate onto the outline of the butterfly, then fill in the wings with loose zigzag lines. Carefully fold the paper so the wings are at right angles, supporting them from underneath in the corner of a large tin or with some other support, and leave until set. Peel away the paper to use.

∾ Chocolate Leaves – Many types of leaf are
suitable, but ensure they are not poisonous before
using. Rose leaves are easy to find and make good
shapes. Wash and dry the leaves carefully before
using. Melt the chocolate, following the instructions
given at the beginning of this section. Using a small
paintbrush, paint a thin layer of chocolate onto the
back of the leaf. Allow to set before adding another
thin layer. When set, carefully peel off the leaf.
Chocolate leaves are also very attractive when
made using two different types of chocolate, white
and dark chocolate, for example. Paint half the
leaf first with one type of chocolate and allow to
set before painting the other half with the second
chocolate. Leave to set, then peel off the leaf
as above.

∾ Chocolate Lace – Make a nonstick baking
parchment piping bag. Draw an outline of the
required shape onto nonstick baking parchment, a
triangle, for example. Pipe chocolate evenly onto
the outline, fill in the centre with lacy squiggles
and leave until set. Remove the paper to use.

∾ Chocolate Squiggles – Use a teaspoon of
melted chocolate to drizzle random shapes onto
nonstick baking parchment. Leave to set and
remove paper to use. Alternatively, pipe a zigzag
line about 5 cm/2 inches long onto a piece of
nonstick baking parchment. Pipe a straight line,
slightly longer at either end, down the middle of
the zigzag.

Handling Chocolate

Chocolate Modelling Paste – Chocolate modelling paste is very useful for cake coverings, as well as for making heavier shapes to decorate your cakes, such as ribbons. To make the paste, simply follow these instructions:

Put 200 g/7 oz dark chocolate in a bowl and add 3 tablespoons of liquid glucose. Set the bowl over a pan of gently simmering water. Stir until the chocolate is just melted, then remove from the heat. Beat until smooth and leave the mixture to cool. When cool enough to handle, knead to a smooth paste on a clean work surface. The mixture can now be rolled and cut to shape. If the paste hardens, wrap it in clingfilm and warm it in the microwave for a few seconds on low.

Caramel and Praline Decorations

Caramel – To make caramel, put 75 g/3 oz granulated sugar into a heavy-based saucepan with about 3 tablespoons cold water. Over a low heat, stir well until the sugar has dissolved completely. If any sugar clings to the pan, brush it down using a wet brush. Bring the mixture to the boil and cook, without stirring, until the mixture turns golden. You may need to tilt the pan carefully to ensure the sugar colours evenly. As soon as the desired colour is reached, remove the pan from the heat and plunge the base of the pan into cold water to stop it from cooking further.

∞ Praline – To make praline, follow the instructions as for caramel, but during the final stage, do not plunge the pan into cold water. Add nuts to the caramel mixture, do not stir, but pour immediately onto an oiled baking sheet. Leave to set at room temperature. Once cold, the praline can be chopped or broken into pieces as required. Keep leftover praline in a sealed container. It will keep for several months if stored this way.

∞ Caramel-dipped Nuts – For caramel-dipped nuts, make the caramel, remove the pan from the heat and plunge into cold water as described earlier. Using two skewers or two forks, dip individual nuts into the hot caramel, lift out carefully, allowing excess to run off, then transfer to a foil-covered tray to set. If the caramel becomes too sticky or starts making a lot of sugar strands, reheat gently until liquid again.

∞ Caramel Shapes – For caramel shapes, make the caramel, remove the pan from the heat and plunge into cold water as described earlier. Using a teaspoon, drizzle or pour spoonfuls of caramel onto an oiled baking sheet. Leave to set before removing from the baking sheet. Do not refrigerate as the shapes will liquefy.

∞ Caramel Lace – To make caramel lace, follow the method for caramel shapes, but use the teaspoon to drizzle threads in a random pattern onto an oiled tray. When set, break into pieces to use as decoration. Do not refrigerate.

Handling Chocolate

Cookies
& Biscuits

You can bake an amazing variety of tasty cookies and biscuits, from classic favourites such as Chocolate Chip Cookies and Gingerbread Biscuits, to fancy, light and delicate Whipped Shortbread. Whether you will be entertaining, catering for a special occasion such as Christmas, or just have a bunch of hungry kids to feed, it's time to roll up your sleeves, step into the kitchen and enter the world of cookies and biscuits.

Cherry Garlands

Makes 30

125 g/4 oz plain flour
pinch salt
65 g/2¹/₂ oz butter, softened
50 g/2 oz caster sugar
1 egg yolk
¹/₂ tsp almond extract

To decorate:

12 glacé cherries
1 egg white, lightly beaten
caster sugar

Preheat the oven to 190°C/375°F/Gas Mark 5 and grease two baking sheets. Sift the flour and salt into a bowl or a food processor, add the butter and rub in with fingertips or process until the mixture resembles fine crumbs. Stir in the sugar.

In another bowl, beat the egg yolk with the almond extract and add to the flour mixture. Stir to make a soft dough, then knead lightly. Roll the dough into pea-size balls and arrange eight balls in a ring on a baking sheet, pressing them together lightly.

Continue making rings until all the dough is used up. Cut each glacé cherry into eight tiny wedges and place three on each biscuit between the balls.

Bake for 14 minutes until golden, remove the biscuits from the oven and brush with beaten egg white. Sprinkle the tops lightly with caster sugar and return to the oven for 2 minutes until a sparkly glaze has formed. Leave to stand on the baking sheets for 2 minutes, then cool completely on a wire rack.

Chocolate Chip Cookies

Makes about 30

130 g/4¹/₂ oz butter
50 g/2 oz caster sugar
65 g/2¹/₂ oz soft dark
brown sugar
1 medium egg, beaten
¹/₂ tsp vanilla extract
125 g/4 oz plain flour
¹/₂ tsp bicarbonate of soda
150 g/5 oz dark or milk
chocolate chips

Preheat the oven to 180°C/350°F/Gas Mark 4, 10 minutes before baking. Lightly butter three or four large baking sheets with 15 g/¹/₂ oz of the butter. Place the remaining butter and both sugars in a food processor and blend until smooth. Add the egg and vanilla extract and blend briefly. Alternatively, cream the butter and sugars together in a bowl, then beat in the egg with the vanilla extract.

If using a food processor, scrape out the mixture with a spatula and place the mixture into a large bowl. Sift the flour and bicarbonate of soda together, then fold into the creamed mixture. When the mixture is blended thoroughly, stir in the chocolate chips.

Drop heaped teaspoons of the mixture onto the prepared baking sheets, spaced well apart, and bake the cookies in the preheated oven for 10–12 minutes until lightly golden.

Leave to cool for a few seconds, then, using a spatula, transfer to a wire rack and cool completely. The cookies are best eaten when just cooked, but can be stored in an airtight container for a few days.

Chewy Choc Nut Cookies

Makes 18

15 g/¹/₂ oz butter
4 medium egg whites
350 g/12 oz icing sugar
75 g/3 oz cocoa powder
2 tbsp plain flour
1 tsp instant coffee powder
125 g/4 oz walnuts,
finely chopped

Preheat the oven to 180°C/350°F/Gas Mark 4, 10 minutes before baking. Lightly butter several baking sheets with the butter and line with a sheet of non-stick baking parchment.

Place the egg whites in a large grease-free bowl and whisk with an electric mixer until the egg whites are very frothy. Add the sugar along with the cocoa powder, flour and coffee powder and whisk again until the ingredients are blended thoroughly. Add 1 tablespoon of water and continue to whisk on the highest speed until the mixture is very thick. Fold in the chopped walnuts.

Place tablespoons of the mixture onto the prepared baking sheets, leaving plenty of space between them as they expand greatly during cooking.

Bake in the preheated oven for 12–15 minutes, or until the tops are firm and quite cracked. Leave to cool for 30 seconds, then using a spatula, transfer to a wire rack and leave to cool. Store in an airtight tin.

Peanut Butter Truffle Cookies

Makes 18

125 g/4 oz plain dark chocolate
150 ml/¼ pint double cream
125 g/4 oz butter or
margarine, softened
125 g/4 oz caster sugar
125 g/4 oz crunchy or smooth
peanut butter
4 tbsp golden syrup
1 tbsp milk
225 g/8 oz plain flour
½ tsp bicarbonate of soda

Preheat the oven to 180°C/350°F/Gas Mark 4, 10 minutes before baking. Make the chocolate filling by breaking the chocolate into small pieces and placing in a heatproof bowl. Put the double cream into a saucepan and heat to boiling point. Immediately pour over the chocolate. Leave to stand for 1–2 minutes, then stir until smooth. Set aside to cool until firm enough to scoop. Do not refrigerate.

Lightly oil a baking sheet. Cream together the butter or margarine and the sugar until light and fluffy. Blend in the peanut butter, followed by the golden syrup and milk.

Sift together the flour and bicarbonate of soda. Add to the peanut butter mixture, mix well and knead until smooth.

Flatten 1–2 tablespoons of the cookie mixture on a chopping board. Put a spoonful of the chocolate mixture into the centre of the cookie dough, then fold the dough around the chocolate to enclose completely.

Put the balls on to the baking sheet and flatten slightly. Bake in the preheated oven for 10–12 minutes until golden. Remove from the oven and transfer to a wire rack to cool completely and serve.

Chocolate Chip Cookies Variation

Makes 36 biscuits

175 g/6 oz plain flour
pinch salt
1 tsp baking powder
1/4 tsp bicarbonate of soda
75 g/3 oz butter or margarine
50 g/2 oz soft light
brown sugar
3 tbsp golden syrup
125 g/4 oz chocolate chips

Preheat the oven to 190°C/375°F/Gas Mark 5, 10 minutes before baking. Lightly oil a large baking sheet.

In a large bowl, sift together the flour, salt, baking powder and bicarbonate of soda. Cut the butter or margarine into small pieces and add to the flour mixture.

Using two knives or the fingertips, rub in the butter or margarine until the mixture resembles coarse breadcrumbs. Add the light brown sugar, golden syrup and chocolate chips. Mix together until a smooth dough forms.

Shape the mixture into small balls and arrange on the baking sheet, leaving enough space to allow them to expand. (These cookies do not increase in size by a great deal, but allow a little space for expansion.)

Flatten the mixture slightly with the fingertips or the heel of the hand. Bake in the preheated oven for 12–15 minutes, or until golden and cooked through.

Allow to cool slightly, then transfer the biscuits on to a wire rack to cool. Serve when cold or otherwise store in an airtight tin.

Traffic Lights

Makes 14

125 g/4 oz butter, softened
75 g/3 oz caster sugar
25 g/1 oz golden syrup
1 medium egg, beaten
few drops vanilla extract
275 g/10 oz plain flour, plus extra
for dusting
1 tsp baking powder

To decorate:

4 tbsp strawberry jam
4 tbsp apricot jam
4 tbsp lime marmalade
icing sugar, for dredging

Preheat the oven to 180°C/350°F/Gas Mark 4. Grease two baking trays. Beat the butter, sugar and syrup together until light and fluffy.

Gradually beat in the egg and vanilla extract. Sift the flour and baking powder into the bowl and stir into the mixture. Gather the mixture up with your hands and work it into a dough. Turn out onto a floured surface and knead gently until smooth. Wrap in clingfilm for 30 minutes and chill.

Roll the pastry out to a thickness of 3 mm/^{1}/$_8$ inch and cut into 28 oblongs measuring 3 x 8.5 cm/1^1/$_4$ x 3^1/$_2$ inches. Using the broad end of a piping nozzle or a cutter measuring 2 cm/^{3}/$_4$ inch wide, cut out three holes in each of 14 of the oblongs, remove the cut-out discs and discard or re-roll to use as pastry trimmings. Place all the oblongs on the baking sheets and bake for 8–10 minutes until golden. Transfer to a wire rack to cool.

Place 3 small teaspoonfuls of different coloured jams along the centre of each rectangular biscuit, starting with strawberry for red at the top, apricot for amber in the middle and lime marmalade for green at the base. Dust the biscuits with the round holes with icing sugar. Position these over the jam on the rectangular biscuits and press down so that the jam shows through.

Oatmeal Raisin Cookies

Makes 24

175 g/6 oz plain flour
150 g/5 oz rolled oats
1 tsp ground ginger
^{1}/$_2$ tsp baking powder
^{1}/$_2$ tsp bicarbonate of soda
125 g/4 oz soft
light brown sugar
50 g/2 oz raisins
1 medium egg,
lightly beaten
150 ml/^{1}/$_4$ pint vegetable
or sunflower oil
4 tbsp milk

Preheat the oven to 200°C/400°F/Gas Mark 6, 15 minutes before baking. Lightly oil a baking sheet.

Mix together the flour, oats, ground ginger, baking powder, bicarbonate of soda, sugar and the raisins in a large bowl.

In another bowl, mix the egg, oil and milk together. Make a well in the centre of the dry ingredients and pour in the egg mixture.

Mix the mixture together well with either a fork or a wooden spoon to make a soft but not sticky dough.

Place spoonfuls of the dough well apart on the oiled baking sheet and flatten the tops down slightly with the tines of a fork. Transfer the biscuits to the preheated oven and bake for 10–12 minutes until golden.

Remove from the oven, leave to cool for 2–3 minutes, then transfer the biscuits to a wire rack to cool. Serve when cold, or otherwise store in an airtight tin.

Whipped Shortbread

Makes 36

225 g/8 oz butter, softened
75 g/3 oz icing sugar
175 g/6 oz plain flour
hundreds and thousands
sugar strands
chocolate drops
silver balls
50 g/2 oz icing sugar
2–3 tsp lemon juice

Preheat the oven to 180°C/350°F/Gas Mark 4, 10 minutes before baking. Lightly oil a baking sheet.

Cream the butter and icing sugar until fluffy. Gradually add the flour and continue beating for a further 2–3 minutes until it is smooth and light.

Roll into balls and place on a baking sheet. Cover half of the dough mixture with hundreds and thousands, sugar strands, chocolate drops or silver balls. Keep the other half plain.

Bake in the preheated oven for 6–8 minutes, until the bottoms are lightly browned. Remove from the oven and transfer to a wire rack to cool.

Sift the icing sugar into a small bowl. Add the lemon juice and blend until a smooth icing forms.

Using a small spoon, swirl the icing over the cooled plain cookies. Decorate with either the extra hundreds and thousands, chocolate drops or silver balls and serve.

Shortbread Thumbs

Makes 12

125 g/4 oz self-raising flour
125 g/4 oz butter, softened
25 g/1 oz white vegetable fat
50 g/2 oz granulated sugar
25 g/1 oz cornflour, sifted
5 tbsp cocoa powder, sifted
125 g/4 oz icing sugar
6 assorted coloured glacé
cherries, rinsed, dried
and halved

Preheat the oven to 150°C/300°F/Gas Mark 2, 10 minutes before baking. Lightly oil two baking sheets. Sift the flour into a large bowl, cut 75 g/3 oz of the butter and the white vegetable fat into small cubes, add to the flour, then, using your fingertips, rub in until the mixture resembles fine breadcrumbs.

Stir in the granulated sugar, sifted cornflour and 4 tablespoons of cocoa powder and bring the mixture together with your hand to form a soft and pliable dough.

Place on a lightly floured surface and shape into 12 small balls. Place onto the baking sheets at least 5 cm/2 inches apart, then press each one with a clean thumb to make a dent.

Bake in the preheated oven for 20–25 minutes or until light golden brown. Remove from the oven and leave for 1–2 minutes to cool. Transfer to a wire rack and leave until cold.

Sift the icing sugar and the remaining cocoa powder into a bowl and add the remaining softened butter. Blend to form a smooth and spreadable icing with 1–2 tablespoons of hot water. Spread a little icing over the top of each biscuit and place half a cherry on each. Leave until set before serving.

Chocolate Orange Biscuits

Makes 30

100 g/3¹/₂ oz dark chocolate
125 g/4 oz butter
125 g/4 oz caster sugar
pinch salt
1 medium egg, beaten
grated zest of 2 oranges
200 g/7 oz plain flour
1 tsp baking powder
125 g/4 oz icing sugar
1–2 tbsp orange juice

Preheat the oven to 200°C/400°F/Gas Mark 6, 15 minutes before baking. Lightly oil several baking sheets. Coarsely grate the chocolate and reserve. Beat the butter and sugar together until creamy. Add the salt, beaten egg and half the orange zest and beat again.

Sift the flour and baking powder, add to the bowl with the grated chocolate and beat to form a dough. Shape into a ball, wrap in clingfilm and chill in the refrigerator for 2 hours.

Roll the dough out on a lightly floured surface to 5 mm/¹/₄ inch thickness and cut into 5 cm/2 inch rounds. Place the rounds on the prepared baking sheets, allowing room for expansion. Bake in the preheated oven for 10–12 minutes until firm. Remove the biscuits from the oven and leave to cool slightly. Using a spatula, transfer to a wire rack and leave to cool.

Sift the icing sugar into a small bowl and stir in sufficient orange juice to make a smooth, spreadable icing. Spread the icing over the biscuits, leave until almost set, then sprinkle on the remaining grated orange zest before serving.

Lemon Butter Biscuits

Makes 14–18

175 g/6 oz butter, softened
75 g/3 oz caster sugar
175 g/6 oz plain flour
75 g/3 oz cornflour
zest of 1 lemon, finely grated
2 tbsp caster sugar, to decorate

Preheat the oven to 170°C/325°F/Gas Mark 3. Grease two baking sheets. Place the butter into a bowl and beat together with the sugar until light and fluffy.

Sift in the flour and cornflour, add the lemon zest and mix together with a flat-bladed knife to form a soft dough.

Place the dough on a lightly floured surface, knead lightly and roll out thinly. Use biscuit cutters to cut out fancy shapes, re-rolling the trimmings to make more biscuits. Carefully lift each biscuit onto a baking sheet with a palette knife, then prick lightly with a fork.

Bake for 12–15 minutes. Cool on the baking sheets for 5 minutes, then place on a wire rack. Once completely cool, dust with caster sugar.

Rum Chocolate Squares

Makes 14–16

125 g/4 oz butter
100 g/3¹/₂ oz caster sugar
pinch salt
2 medium egg yolks
225 g/8 oz plain flour
50 g/2 oz cornflour
¹/₄ tsp baking powder
2 tbsp cocoa powder
1 tbsp rum

Preheat the oven to 190°C/375°F/Gas Mark 5, 10 minutes before baking. Lightly oil several baking sheets. Cream the butter, sugar and salt together in a large bowl until light and fluffy. Add the egg yolks and beat well until smooth.

Sift together 175 g/6 oz of the flour, the cornflour and the baking powder, add to the mixture and mix well with a wooden spoon until a soft, smooth dough is formed.

Halve the dough and knead the cocoa powder into one half and the rum and the remaining plain flour into the other half. Place the two mixtures in two separate bowls, cover with clingfilm and chill in the refrigerator for 1 hour.

Roll out both pieces of dough separately on a well-floured surface into two thin rectangles about 5 mm/¹/₄ inch thick. Place one on top of the other, cut out squares approximately 5 cm/2 inch square and place on the prepared baking sheets.

Bake in the preheated oven, half with the chocolate uppermost and the other half rum side up, for 10–12 minutes until firm. Remove from the oven and leave to cool slightly. Using a spatula, transfer to a wire rack and leave to cool, then serve.

Palmier Biscuits with Apple Purée

Makes 20

250 g/9 oz prepared puff pastry,
thawed if frozen
40 g/1¹/₂ oz caster sugar
25 g/1 oz icing sugar
1 tsp ground cinnamon
¹/₄ tsp ground ginger
¹/₄ tsp freshly grated nutmeg
450 g/1 lb Bramley cooking
apples, roughly chopped
50 g/2 oz granulated or
caster sugar
25 g/1 oz raisins
25 g/1 oz dried cherries
zest of 1 orange
double cream, lightly whipped,
to serve

Preheat the oven to 200°C/400°F/Gas Mark 6, 15 minutes before baking. Roll out the pastry on a lightly floured surface to form a 25.5 x 30.5 cm/ 10 x 12 inch rectangle. Trim the edges with a small sharp knife. Sift together the caster sugar, icing sugar, cinnamon, ginger and nutmeg into a bowl. Generously dust both sides of the pastry sheet with about a quarter of the mixture. With a long edge facing the body, fold either side halfway towards the centre. Dust with a third of the remaining mixture. Fold each side again so that they almost meet in the centre and dust again with about half the remaining mixture. Fold the two sides together down the centre of the pastry to give six layers. Wrap in clingfilm and refrigerate for 1–2 hours until firm. Reserve the remaining spiced sugar.

Remove the pastry from the refrigerator, unwrap and roll in the remaining sugar to give a good coating all round. Using a sharp knife, cut the roll into about 20 thin slices. Place the cut side down on to a baking sheet and place in the pre-heated oven. Cook for 10 minutes, turn the biscuits over and cook for a further 5–10 minutes, or until golden and crisp. Remove from the oven and transfer to a wire rack. Allow to cool completely.

Meanwhile, combine the remaining ingredients in a saucepan. Cover and cook gently for 15 minutes until the apple is completely soft. Stir well and allow to cool. Serve the palmiers with a spoonful of the apple purée and a little of the whipped double cream

Chocolate Shortcakes

Makes 30–32

225 g/8 oz unsalted
butter, softened
150 g/5 oz icing sugar
1 tsp vanilla extract
250 g/9 oz plain flour
25 g/1 oz cocoa powder
$^1/_4$ tsp salt
extra icing sugar,
to decorate

Preheat the oven to 170°C/325°F/Gas Mark 3, 10 minutes before baking. Lightly oil several baking sheets and line with nonstick baking parchment. Place the butter, icing sugar and vanilla extract together in a food processor and blend briefly until smooth. Alternatively, using a wooden spoon, cream the butter, icing sugar and vanilla extract in a large bowl.

Sift the flour, cocoa powder and salt together, then either add to the food processor bowl and blend quickly to form a dough, or add to the bowl and, using your hands, mix together until a smooth dough is formed.

Turn the dough out onto a clean board lined with clingfilm. Place another sheet of clingfilm over the top and roll the dough out until it is 1 cm/$^1/_2$ inch thick. Transfer the whole board to the refrigerator and chill for 1$^1/_2$–2 hours.

Remove the top piece of clingfilm and use a 5 cm/2 inch cutter to cut the dough into 30–32 rounds. Place the rounds on the prepared baking sheets and bake in the preheated oven for about 15 minutes until firm.

Cool for 1 minute, then, using a spatula, carefully remove the shortcakes from the baking parchment and transfer to a wire rack. Leave to cool completely. Sprinkle the shortcakes with sifted icing sugar before serving. Store in an airtight container for a few days.

Coconut Macaroons

Makes 18

rice paper
2 medium egg whites
125 g/4 oz icing sugar
125 g/4 oz desiccated coconut
125 g/4 oz ground almonds
zest of $\frac{1}{2}$ lemon or lime,
finely grated

Preheat the oven to 180°C/350°F/Gas Mark 4. Line two baking sheets with rice paper.

Whisk the egg whites in a clean, dry bowl until soft peaks form. Using a large metal spoon, fold in the icing sugar. Fold in the coconut, almonds and lemon or lime zest until a sticky dough forms.

Heap dessertspoonfuls of the mixture onto the rice paper on the baking sheets. Bake for 10 minutes, then reduce the oven temperature to 150°C/300°F/Gas Mark 2.

Bake for a further 5–8 minutes until firm and golden, then remove to a wire rack to cool, breaking off any excess rice paper.

Chocolate Macaroons

Makes 20

65 g/2¹/₂ oz dark chocolate
125 g/4 oz ground almonds
125 g/4 oz caster sugar
¹/₄ tsp almond extract
1 tbsp cocoa powder
2 medium egg whites
1 tbsp icing sugar

Preheat the oven to 180°C/350°F/Gas Mark 4, 10 minutes before baking. Lightly oil several baking sheets and line with sheets of nonstick baking parchment. Melt the chocolate in a heatproof bowl set over a saucepan of simmering water. Alternatively, melt in the microwave according to the manufacturer's instructions. Stir until smooth, then cool slightly.

Place the ground almonds in a food processor and add the sugar, almond extract, cocoa powder and one of the egg whites. Add the melted chocolate and a little of the other egg white and blend to make a soft, smooth paste. Alternatively, place the ground almonds with the sugar, almond extract and cocoa powder in a bowl and make a well in the centre. Add the melted chocolate with sufficient egg white and gradually blend together to form a smooth but not sticky paste.

Shape the dough into small balls the size of large walnuts and place them on the prepared baking sheets. Flatten them slightly, then brush with a little water. Sprinkle over a little icing sugar and bake in the preheated oven for 10–12 minutes until just firm.

Using a spatula, carefully lift the macaroons off the baking parchment and transfer to a wire rack to cool. These are best served immediately, but can be stored in an airtight container.

Almond Macaroons

Makes 12

rice paper
125 g/4 oz caster sugar
50 g/2 oz ground almonds
1 tsp ground rice
2–3 drops almond essence
1 medium egg white
8 blanched almonds, halved

Preheat the oven to 150°C/300°F/Gas Mark 2, 10 minutes before baking. Line a baking sheet with the rice paper.

Mix the caster sugar, ground almonds, ground rice and almond essence together and reserve.

Whisk the egg white until stiff then gently fold in the caster sugar mixture with a metal spoon or rubber spatula.

Mix to form a stiff but not sticky paste. If the mixture is very sticky, add a little extra ground almonds. Place small spoonfuls of the mixture, about the size of an apricot, well apart on the rice paper.

Place a half-blanched almond in the centre of each. Place in the preheated oven and bake for 25 minutes, or until just pale golden.

Remove the biscuits from the oven and leave to cool for a few minutes on the baking sheet. Cut or tear the rice paper around the macaroons to release them. Once cold, serve them or store in an airtight tin.

Chocolate Nut Refrigerator Biscuits

Makes 18

165 g/5^1/$_2$ oz slightly
salted butter
150 g/5 oz soft dark
brown sugar
25 g/1 oz granulated sugar
1 medium egg, beaten
200 g/7 oz plain flour
^{1}/$_2$ tsp bicarbonate of soda
25 g/1 oz cocoa powder
125 g/4 oz pecan nuts,
finely chopped

Preheat the oven to 190˚C/375˚F/Gas Mark 5, 10 minutes before baking. Lightly grease several baking sheets with 15 g/^{1}/$_2$ oz of the butter. Cream the remaining butter and both sugars in a large bowl until light and fluffy, then gradually beat in the egg.

Sift the flour, bicarbonate of soda and cocoa powder together, then gradually fold into the creamed mixture together with the chopped pecans. Mix thoroughly until a smooth but stiff dough is formed.

Place the dough on a lightly floured surface or pastry board and roll into sausage shapes about 5 cm/2 inches in diameter. Wrap in clingfilm and chill in the refrigerator for at least 12 hours, or preferably overnight.

Cut the dough into thin slices and place on the prepared baking sheets. Bake in the preheated oven for 8–10 minutes until firm. Remove from the oven and leave to cool slightly. Using a spatula, transfer to a wire rack to cool. Store in an airtight container.

Melting Moments

Makes 16

125 g/4 oz butter, softened
75 g/3 oz caster sugar
1/2 tsp vanilla extract
150 g/5 oz self-raising flour
pinch salt
1 small egg or 1/2 medium egg, beaten
25 g/1 oz porridge oats
4 glacé cherries, quartered

Preheat the oven to 180°C/350°F/Gas Mark 4. Grease two baking sheets.

Beat the butter until light and fluffy, then whisk in the caster sugar and vanilla extract. Sift the flour and salt into the bowl. Add the egg and mix to a soft dough.

Break the dough into 16 pieces and roll each piece into a ball. Spread the oats out on a small flat bowl or plate. Roll each ball in the oats to coat them all over without flattening them.

Place a cherry quarter in the centre of each ball, then place on the baking sheets, spaced well apart. Bake for about 15 minutes until risen and golden. Remove from the baking sheets with a palette knife and cool on a wire rack.

Honey Chocolate Hearts

Makes about 20

65 g/2¹/₂ oz caster sugar
15 g/¹/₂ oz butter
125 g/4 oz thick honey
1 small egg, beaten
pinch salt
1 tbsp mixed peel or chopped glacé ginger
¹/₄ tsp ground cinnamon
pinch ground cloves
225 g/8 oz plain flour, sifted
¹/₂ tsp baking powder, sifted
75 g/3 oz milk chocolate

Preheat the oven to 220°C/425°F/Gas Mark 7, 15 minutes before baking. Lightly oil two baking sheets. Heat the sugar, butter and honey together in a small saucepan until everything has melted and the mixture is smooth.

Remove from the heat and stir until slightly cooled, then add the beaten egg with the salt and beat well. Stir in the mixed peel or glacé ginger, ground cinnamon, ground cloves, the flour and the baking powder and mix well until a dough is formed. Wrap in clingfilm and chill in the refrigerator for 45 minutes.

Place the chilled dough on a lightly floured surface, roll out to about 5 mm/¹/₄ inch thickness and cut out small heart shapes. Place onto the prepared baking sheets and bake in the oven for 8–10 minutes. Remove from the oven and leave to cool slightly. Using a spatula, transfer to a wire rack until cold.

Melt the chocolate in a heatproof bowl set over a saucepan of simmering water. Alternatively, melt the chocolate in the microwave according to the manufacturer's instructions, until smooth. Dip one half of each biscuit in the melted chocolate. Leave to set before serving.

Ginger Snaps

Makes 40

300 g/11 oz butter or
margarine, softened
225 g/8 oz soft light
brown sugar
75 g/3 oz black treacle
1 medium egg
400 g/14 oz plain flour
2 tsp bicarbonate of soda
$1/2$ tsp salt
1 tsp ground ginger
1 tsp ground cloves
1 tsp ground cinnamon
50 g/2 oz granulated sugar

Preheat the oven to 190°C/375°F/Gas Mark 5, 10 minutes before baking. Lightly oil a baking sheet.

Cream together the butter or margarine and the sugar until light and fluffy.

Warm the treacle in the microwave for 30–40 seconds, then add gradually to the butter mixture with the egg. Beat until combined well.

In a separate bowl, sift the flour, bicarbonate of soda, salt, ground ginger, ground cloves and ground cinnamon. Add to the butter mixture and mix together to form a firm dough.

Chill in the refrigerator for 1 hour. Shape the dough into small balls and roll in the granulated sugar. Place well apart on the oiled baking sheet.

Sprinkle the baking sheet with a little water and transfer to the preheated oven.

Bake for 12 minutes, until golden and crisp. Transfer to a wire rack to cool and serve.

Gingerbread Biscuits

Makes 20 large or 28 small biscuits

225 g/8 oz plain flour, plus extra
for dusting
$^1/_2$ tsp ground ginger
$^1/_2$ tsp mixed spice
$^1/_2$ tsp bicarbonate of soda
75 g/3 oz butter
2 tbsp golden syrup
1 tbsp black treacle
75 g/3 oz soft dark
brown sugar
50 g/2 oz royal icing sugar,
to decorate

Preheat the oven to 180°C/350°F/Gas Mark 4 and grease two baking sheets. Sift the flour, spices and bicarbonate of soda into a bowl.

Place the butter, syrup, treacle and sugar in a heavy-based pan with 1 tablespoon water and heat gently until every grain of sugar has dissolved and the butter has melted. Cool for 5 minutes, then pour the melted mixture into the dry ingredients and mix to a soft dough.

Leave the dough, covered, for 30 minutes. Roll out the dough on a lightly floured surface to a 3 mm/$^1/_8$ inch thickness and cut out fancy shapes. Gather up the trimmings and re-roll the dough, cutting out more shapes. Place on the baking sheets using a palette knife and bake for about 10 minutes until golden and firm. Be careful not to overcook, as the biscuits will brown quickly.

Decorate the biscuits by mixing the royal icing sugar with enough water to make a piping consistency. Place the icing in a small paper piping bag with the end snipped away and pipe faces and decorations onto the biscuits.

Chocolate Ginger Florentines

Makes 14–16

40 g/1¹/₂ oz butter
5 tbsp double cream
50 g/2 oz caster sugar
65 g/2¹/₂ oz chopped almonds
25 g/1 oz flaked almonds
40 g/1¹/₂ oz glacé
ginger, chopped
25 g/1 oz plain flour
pinch salt
150 g/5 oz dark chocolate

Preheat the oven to 180°C/350°F/Gas Mark 4, 10 minutes before baking. Lightly oil several baking sheets.

Melt the butter, cream and sugar together in a saucepan and bring slowly to the boil. Remove from the heat and stir in the almonds and the glacé ginger.

Leave to cool slightly, then mix in the flour and the salt. Blend together, then place heaped teaspoons of the mixture on the baking sheets. Make sure they are spaced well apart, as they expand during cooking. Flatten them slightly with the back of a wet spoon.

Bake in the preheated oven for 10–12 minutes until just brown at the edges. Leave to cool slightly. Using a spatula, carefully transfer to a wire rack and leave to cool.

Melt the chocolate in a heatproof bowl set over a saucepan of gently simmering water. Alternatively, melt the chocolate in the microwave according to the manufacturer's instructions, until just liquid and smooth. Spread thickly over one side of the Florentines, then mark wavy lines through the chocolate using a fork and leave until firm.

Chocolate Florentines

Makes 20

125 g/4 oz butter or margarine
125 g/4 oz soft light
brown sugar
1 tbsp double cream
50 g/2 oz blanched almonds,
roughly chopped
50 g/2 oz hazelnuts,
roughly chopped
75 g/3 oz sultanas
50 g/2 oz glacé cherries,
roughly chopped
50 g/2 oz dark chocolate, roughly
chopped or broken
50 g/2 oz milk chocolate, roughly
chopped or broken
50 g/2 oz white chocolate, roughly
chopped or broken

Preheat the oven to 180°C/350°F/Gas Mark 4, 10 minutes before baking. Lightly oil a baking sheet.

Melt the butter or margarine with the sugar and double cream in a small saucepan over a very low heat. Do not boil. Remove from the heat and stir in the almonds, hazelnuts, sultanas and cherries.

Drop teaspoonfuls of the mixture onto the baking sheet. Transfer to the preheated oven and bake for 10 minutes, or until golden. Leave the biscuits to cool on the baking sheet for about 5 minutes, then carefully transfer to a wire rack to cool.

Melt the dark, milk and white chocolates in separate bowls, either in the microwave, following the manufacturer's instructions, or in a small bowl placed over a saucepan of gently simmering water.

Spread one third of the biscuits with the dark chocolate, one third with the milk chocolate and one third with the white chocolate. When almost set, mark out wavy lines on the chocolate with the tines of a fork. Alternatively, dip some of the biscuits in chocolate to half coat and serve.

White Chocolate Cookies

Makes about 24

130 g/4^1/$_2$ oz butter
40 g/1^1/$_2$ oz caster sugar
65 g/2^1/$_2$ oz soft dark
brown sugar
1 medium egg
125 g/4 oz plain flour
^{1}/$_2$ tsp bicarbonate of soda
few drops vanilla extract
150 g/5 oz white chocolate
50 g/2 oz whole
hazelnuts, shelled

Preheat the oven to 180°C/350°F/Gas Mark 4, 10 minutes before baking. Lightly grease several baking sheets with 15 g/^{1}/$_2$ oz of the butter.

Place the remaining butter with both sugars into a large bowl and beat with a wooden spoon or an electric mixer until soft and fluffy. Beat the egg, then gradually beat into the creamed mixture. Sift the flour and the bicarbonate of soda together, then carefully fold into the creamed mixture with a few drops of vanilla extract.

Roughly chop the chocolate and hazelnuts into small pieces, add to the bowl and gently stir into the mixture. Mix together lightly to blend.

Spoon heaped teaspoons of the mixture onto the prepared baking sheets, making sure that there is plenty of space in between each one, as they will spread a lot during cooking.

Bake the cookies in the preheated oven for 10 minutes, or until golden, then remove from the oven and leave to cool for 1 minute. Using a spatula, carefully transfer to a wire rack and leave to cool completely. The cookies are best eaten on the day they are made. Store in an airtight container.

Chocolate Vanilla Rings

Makes 26

175 g/6 oz butter, softened
125 g/4 oz caster sugar
few drops vanilla extract
250 g/9 oz plain flour
15 g/¹/₂ oz cocoa powder
25 g/1 oz ground almonds

Preheat the oven to 180°C/350°F/Gas Mark 4 and grease two baking sheets.

Put the butter and sugar in a bowl and beat until light and fluffy. Add the vanilla extract, sift in the flour and mix to a soft dough. Divide the dough in two and add the cocoa powder to one half and the almonds to the other.

Knead each piece of dough separately into a smooth ball, wrap and chill for 30 minutes. Divide each piece into 26 pieces. Take one dark and one light ball and roll each separately into ropes about 12.5 cm/5 inches long using your fingers.

Twist the ropes together to form a circlet and pinch the ends together. Repeat with the remaining dough and place on a greased baking sheet. Bake for 12–14 minutes until risen and firm. Remove to cool on a wire rack.

Chocolate Hazelnut Cookies

Makes 12

75 g/3 oz blanched hazelnuts
100 g/3¹/₂ oz caster sugar
50 g/2 oz unsalted butter
pinch salt
5 tsp cocoa powder
3 tbsp double cream
2 large egg whites
40 g/1¹/₂ oz plain flour
2 tbsp rum
75 g/3 oz white chocolate

Preheat the oven to 180°C/350°F/Gas Mark 4, 10 minutes before baking. Lightly oil and flour two or three baking sheets. Chop 25 g/1 oz of the hazelnuts and reserve. Blend the remaining hazelnuts with the caster sugar in a food processor until finely ground. Add the butter to the processor bowl and blend until pale and creamy.

Add the salt, cocoa powder and the double cream and mix well. Scrape the mixture into a bowl, using a spatula, and stir in the egg whites. Sift the flour, then stir into the mixture together with the rum.

Spoon heaped tablespoons of the batter onto the baking sheets and sprinkle over a few of the reserved hazelnuts. Bake in the preheated oven for 5–7 minutes or until firm. Remove the cookies from the oven and leave to cool for 1–2 minutes. Using a spatula, transfer to wire racks and leave to cool.

When the biscuits are cold, melt the chocolate in a heatproof bowl set over a saucepan of simmering water. Stir until smooth, then drizzle a little of the chocolate over the top of each biscuit. Leave to dry on a wire rack before serving.

Chocolate Almond Biscuits

Makes 18–20

130 g/4^1/$_2$ oz butter
65 g/2^1/$_2$ oz icing sugar
1 medium egg, beaten
1 tbsp milk
grated zest of 1 lemon
250 g/9 oz plain flour
100 g/3^1/$_2$ oz blanched
almonds, chopped
125 g/4 oz dark chocolate
75 g/3 oz flaked
almonds, toasted

Preheat the oven to 200°C/400°F/Gas Mark 6, 15 minutes before baking. Lightly oil several baking sheets.

Cream the butter and icing sugar together until light and fluffy, then gradually beat in the egg, beating well after each addition. When all the egg has been added, stir in the milk and lemon zest. Sift the flour, then stir into the mixture together with the chopped almonds to form a smooth and pliable dough. Wrap in clingfilm and chill in the refrigerator for 2 hours.

Roll the dough out on a lightly floured surface, in a large oblong about 5 mm/^{1}/$_4$ inch thick. Cut into strips about 6.5 cm/2^1/$_2$ inches long and 4 cm/1^1/$_2$ inches wide and place on the prepared baking sheets.

Bake in the preheated oven for 15 minutes, or until golden, then remove from the oven and leave to cool for a few minutes. Transfer to a wire rack and leave to cool completely.

Melt the chocolate in a heatproof bowl set over a saucepan of simmering water. Alternatively, the chocolate can be melted in the microwave according to the manufacturer's instructions, until smooth. Spread the chocolate thickly over the biscuits, sprinkle over the toasted flaked almonds and leave to set before serving.

Chequered Biscuits

Makes 20

150 g/5 oz butter
75 g/3 oz icing sugar
pinch salt
200 g/7 oz plain flour
25 g/1 oz cocoa powder
1 small egg white

Preheat the oven to 190°C/375°F/Gas Mark 5, 10 minutes before baking. Lightly oil three or four baking sheets. Place the butter and icing sugar in a bowl and cream together until light and fluffy.

Add the salt, then gradually add the flour, beating well after each addition. Mix well to form a firm dough. Cut the dough in half and knead the cocoa powder into one half. Wrap both portions of dough separately in clingfilm and then leave to chill in the refrigerator for 2 hours.

Divide each piece of dough into three portions. Roll each portion of dough into a long roll and arrange these rolls on top of each other to form a chequerboard design, sealing them with egg white. Wrap in clingfilm and refrigerate for 1 hour.

Cut the dough into 5 mm/$^1/_4$ inch thick slices, place on the baking sheets and bake in the preheated oven for 10–15 minutes. Remove from the oven, and leave to cool for a few minutes. Transfer to a wire rack and leave until cold before serving. Store in an airtight tin.

Golden Honey Fork Biscuits

Makes 20–24 biscuits

125 g/4 oz butter or block
margarine, diced
125 g/4 oz soft light
brown sugar
1 medium egg, beaten
1/2 tsp vanilla extract
2 tbsp clear honey
200 g/7 oz plain flour
1/2 tsp baking powder
1/2 tsp ground cinnamon

Preheat the oven to 180°C/350°F/Gas Mark 4. Grease two baking sheets.

Place the butter and sugar in a bowl and beat together until light and fluffy. Beat in the egg, a little at a time, and then beat in the vanilla extract and honey.

Sift the flour, baking powder and cinnamon into the bowl and fold into the mixture with a large metal spoon.

Put heaped teaspoons of the mixture onto the prepared baking sheets, leaving room for them to spread out during baking. Press the top of each round with the tines of a fork to make a light indentation.

Bake for 10–12 minutes until golden. Cool for 2 minutes on the baking sheets, then transfer to a wire rack to cool completely.

Coconut Almond Munchies

Makes 26-30

5 medium egg whites
250 g/9 oz icing sugar, plus extra
to sprinkle
225 g/8 oz ground almonds
200 g/7 oz desiccated coconut
grated rind of 1 lemon
125 g/4 oz milk chocolate
125 g/4 oz white chocolate

Preheat the oven to 150°C/300°F/Gas Mark 2, 10 minutes before baking. Line several baking sheets with rice paper. Place the egg whites in a clean, grease-free bowl and whisk until stiff and standing in peaks. Sift the icing sugar, then carefully fold half of the sugar into the whisked egg whites together with the ground almonds. Add the coconut, the remaining icing sugar and the lemon rind and mix together to form a very sticky dough.

Place the mixture in a piping bag and pipe the mixture into walnut-sized mounds onto the rice paper, then sprinkle with a little extra icing sugar. Bake in the preheated oven for 20–25 minutes, or until set and golden on the outside. Remove from the oven and leave to cool slightly. Using a spatula, carefully transfer to a wire rack and leave until cold.

Break the milk and white chocolate into pieces and place in two separate bowls. Melt both chocolates set over saucepans of gently simmering water. Alternatively, melt in the microwave, according to the manufacturer's instructions. Stir until smooth and free from lumps. Dip one edge of each munchie in the milk chocolate and leave to dry on non-stick baking parchment. When dry, dip the other side into the white chocolate. Leave to set, then serve as soon as possible.

Oatmeal Coconut Cookies

Makes 40

225 g/8 oz butter
or margarine
125 g/4 oz soft light
brown sugar
125 g/4 oz caster sugar
1 large egg, lightly beaten
1 tsp vanilla essence
225 g/8 oz plain flour
1 tsp baking powder
1/2 tsp bicarbonate of soda
125 g/4 oz rolled oats
75 g/3 oz desiccated coconut

Preheat the oven to 180°C/350°F/Gas Mark 4, 10 minutes before baking. Lightly oil a baking sheet.

Cream together the butter or margarine and sugars until light and fluffy. Gradually stir in the egg and vanilla essence and beat until well blended.

Sift together the flour, baking powder and bicarbonate of soda in another bowl. Add to the butter and sugar mixture and beat together until smooth. Fold in the rolled oats and coconut with a metal spoon or rubber spatula.

Roll heaped teaspoonfuls of the mixture into balls and place on the baking sheet about 5 cm/2 inches apart and flatten each ball slightly with the heel of the hand.

Transfer to the preheated oven and bake for 12–15 minutes, until just golden.

Remove from the oven and transfer the biscuits to wire rack to cool completely before serving.

Pumpkin Cookies

Makes 48

125 g/4 oz butter, softened
150 g/5 oz plain flour
175 g/6 oz soft light brown sugar,
lightly packed
225 g/8 oz canned pumpkin or
cooked pumpkin
1 medium egg, beaten
2 tsp ground cinnamon
2^1/$_2$ tsp vanilla essence
^{1}/$_2$ tsp baking powder
^{1}/$_2$ tsp bicarbonate of soda
^{1}/$_2$ tsp freshly grated nutmeg
125 g/4 oz wholemeal flour
75 g/3 oz pecans,
roughly chopped
100 g/3^1/$_2$ oz raisins
50 g/2 oz unsalted butter
225 g/8 oz icing sugar
2 tbsp milk

Preheat the oven to 190˚C/375˚F/Gas Mark 5, 10 minutes before baking. Lightly oil a baking sheet and reserve.

Using an electric mixer, beat the butter until light and fluffy. Add the flour, sugar, pumpkin, beaten egg and beat with the mixer until mixed well.

Stir in the ground cinnamon, 1 teaspoon of the vanilla essence and then sift in the baking powder, bicarbonate of soda and grated nutmeg. Beat the mixture until combined well, scraping down the sides of the bowl.

Add the wholemeal flour, chopped nuts and raisins to the mixture and fold in with a metal spoon or rubber spatula until mixed thoroughly together. Place teaspoonfuls about 5 cm/2 inches apart on to the baking sheet. Bake in the pre-heated oven for 10–12 minutes, or until the cookie edges are firm.

Remove the biscuits from the oven and leave to cool on a wire rack. Meanwhile, melt the butter in a small saucepan over a medium heat, until pale and just turning golden brown. Remove from the heat. Add the sugar, remaining vanilla essence and milk, stirring. Drizzle over the cooled cookies and serve.

Viennese Fingers

Makes 28

225 g/8 oz butter, softened
75 g/3 oz icing sugar
1 medium egg, beaten
1 tsp vanilla extract
275 g/10 oz plain flour
1/2 tsp baking powder

To decorate:

4 tbsp sieved apricot jam
225 g/8 oz plain chocolate

Preheat the oven to 180°C/350°F/Gas Mark 4. Grease two baking sheets. Put the butter and icing sugar in a bowl and beat together until soft and fluffy.

Whisk in the egg and vanilla extract with 1 tablespoon of the flour. Sift in the remaining flour and the baking powder and beat with a wooden spoon to make a soft dough.

Place the mixture in a piping bag fitted with a large star nozzle and pipe into 6.5 cm/2¹/₂ inch lengths on the baking sheets. Bake for 15–20 minutes until pale golden and firm, then transfer to a wire rack to cool.

When cold, thinly spread one flat side of a biscuit with apricot jam and sandwich together with another biscuit.

To decorate the biscuits, break the chocolate into squares and place in a heatproof bowl and stand this over a pan of simmering water. Stir until the chocolate has melted, then dip the ends of the biscuits into the chocolate to coat. Leave on a wire rack for 1 hour until set.

Chocolate Whirls

Makes 20

125 g/4 oz soft margarine
75 g/3 oz unsalted
butter, softened
75 g/3 oz icing sugar, sifted
75 g/3 oz dark chocolate,
melted and cooled
15 g/¹/₂ oz cornflour, sifted
125 g/4 oz plain flour
125 g/4 oz self-raising flour

For the buttercream

125 g/4 oz unsalted
butter, softened
¹/₂ tsp vanilla extract
225 g/8 oz icing sugar, sifted

Preheat the oven to 180°C/350°F/Gas Mark 4, 10 minutes before baking. Lightly oil two baking sheets.

Cream the margarine, butter and icing sugar together until the mixture is light and fluffy. Stir the chocolate until smooth, then beat into the creamed mixture. Stir in the cornflour. Sift the flours together, then gradually add to the creamed mixture, a little at a time, beating well after each addition. Beat until the consistency is smooth and stiff enough for piping.

Put the mixture in a piping bag fitted with a large star nozzle and pipe 40 small whirls onto the prepared baking sheets. Bake the whirls in the preheated oven for 12–15 minutes until firm to the touch. Remove from the oven and leave to cool for about 2 minutes. Using a spatula, transfer the whirls to wire racks and leave to cool.

Meanwhile, make the buttercream. Cream the butter with the vanilla extract until soft. Gradually beat in the icing sugar and add a little cooled boiled water if necessary, to give a smooth consistency. When the whirls are cold, pipe or spread on the prepared buttercream, sandwich together and serve.

Italian Biscotti

Makes 26–28 Biscuits

150 g/5 oz butter
200 g/7 oz caster sugar
$^1/_4$ tsp vanilla essence
1 small egg, beaten
$^1/_4$ tsp ground cinnamon
grated rind of 1 lemon
15 g/ $^1/_2$ oz ground almonds
150 g/5 oz plain flour
150 g/5 oz plain dark chocolate

Preheat the oven to 190°C/375°F/Gas Mark 5, 10 minutes before baking. Lightly oil three or four baking sheets and reserve. Cream the butter and sugar together in a bowl and mix in the vanilla essence. When it is light and fluffy beat in the egg with the cinnamon, lemon rind and the ground almonds. Stir in the flour to make a firm dough.

Knead lightly until smooth and free from cracks. Shape the dough into rectangular blocks about 4 cm/1$^1/_2$ inches in diameter, wrap in greaseproof paper and chill in the refrigerator for at least 2 hours.

Cut the chilled dough into 5 mm/$^1/_4$ inch slices, place on the baking sheets and cook in the preheated oven for 12–15 minutes or until firm. Remove from the oven, cool slightly, then transfer to wire racks to cool.

When completely cold, melt the chocolate in a heatproof bowl set over a saucepan of simmering water. Alternatively, melt the chocolate in the microwave according to the manufacturer's instructions. Spoon into a piping bag and pipe over the biscuits. Leave to dry on a sheet of nonstick baking parchment before serving.

Cantuccini

Makes 24 biscuits

250 g/9 oz plain flour
250 g/9 oz caster sugar
$^1/_2$ tsp baking powder
$^1/_2$ tsp vanilla essence
2 medium eggs
1 medium egg yolk
100 g/3$^1/_2$ oz mixed almonds and
hazelnuts, toasted and
roughly chopped
1 tsp whole aniseed
1 medium egg yolk mixed with
1 tbsp water, to glaze
Vin Santo or coffee, to serve

Preheat oven to 180°C/350°F/Gas Mark 4. Line a large baking sheet with non-stick baking parchment. Place the flour, caster sugar, baking powder, vanilla essence, the whole eggs and one of the egg yolks into a food processor and blend until the mixture forms a ball, scraping down the sides once or twice. Turn the mixture out on to a lightly floured surface and knead in the chopped nuts and aniseed.

Divide the paste into three pieces and roll into logs about 4 cm/ 1$^1/_2$ inches wide. Place the logs on to the baking sheet at least 5 cm/2 inches apart. Brush lightly with the other egg yolk beaten with 1 tablespoon of water and bake in the preheated oven for 30–35 minutes.

Remove from the oven and reduce the oven temperature to 150°C/300°F/Gas Mark 2. Cut the logs diagonally into 2.5 cm/ 1 inch slices and lay cut-side down on the baking sheet. Return to the oven for a further 30–40 minutes, or until dry and firm. Cool on a wire rack and store in an airtight container. Serve with Vin Santo or coffee.

Almond Pistachio Biscotti

Makes 12 biscuits

125 g/4 oz ground almonds
50 g/2 oz shelled pistachios
50 g/2 oz blanched almonds
2 medium eggs
1 medium egg yolk
125 g/4 oz icing sugar
225 g/8 oz plain flour
1 tsp baking powder
pinch salt
zest of 1/2 lemon

Preheat oven to 180°C/350°F/Gas Mark 4. Line a large baking sheet with non-stick baking parchment. Toast the ground almonds and whole nuts lightly and reserve until cool.

Beat together the eggs, egg yolk and icing sugar until thick, then beat in the flour, baking powder and salt. Add the lemon zest, ground almonds and whole nuts and mix to form a slightly sticky dough.

Turn the dough on to a lightly floured surface and, using lightly floured hands, form into a log measuring approximately 30 cm/ 12 inches long. Place down the centre of the prepared baking sheet and transfer to the preheated oven. Bake for 20 minutes.

Remove from the oven and increase the oven temperature to 200°C/400°F/Gas Mark 6. Cut the log diagonally into 2.5 cm/ 1 inch slices. Return to the baking sheet, cut-side down and bake for a further 10–15 minutes until golden, turning once after 10 minutes. Leave to cool on a wire rack and store in an airtight container.

Brownies,

Traybakes

 Loaf Cakes

If you've got a party or picnic coming up, what better way to bake up a storm than in the form of brownies and traybakes? Simple, versatile and an ideal way to satisfy a whole host of hungry mouths, these recipes will give great tasting results time and again. From indulgent classics such as Chocolate Fudge Brownies and Marbled Toffee Shortbread to fruity favourites like Apricot & Almond Slice, there is something to suit every taste.

Chocolate Nut Brownies

Makes 16

125 g/4 oz butter
150 g/5 oz firmly packed soft light
brown sugar
50 g/2 oz dark chocolate, roughly
chopped or broken
2 tbsp smooth peanut butter
2 medium eggs
50 g/2 oz unsalted roasted
peanuts, finely chopped
100 g/3½ oz self-raising flour

For the topping

125 g/4 oz dark chocolate, roughly
chopped or broken
50 ml/2 fl oz sour cream

Preheat the oven to 180°C/350°F/Gas Mark 4, 10 minutes before baking. Lightly oil and line a 20.5 cm/8 inch, square cake tin with greaseproof paper.

Place the butter, sugar and chocolate in a small saucepan and heat gently until the sugar and chocolate have melted, stirring constantly. Reserve and cool slightly.

Mix together the peanut butter, eggs and peanuts in a large bowl. Stir in the cooled chocolate mixture. Sift in the flour and fold together with a metal spoon or rubber spatula until combined.

Pour into the prepared tin and bake in the preheated oven for about 30 minutes until just firm. Cool for 5 minutes in the tin before turning out onto a wire rack to cool.

To make the topping, melt the chocolate in a heatproof bowl over a saucepan of gently simmering water, making sure that the base of the bowl does not touch the water.

Cool slightly, then stir in the sour cream until smooth and glossy. Spread over the brownies, refrigerate until set, then cut into squares. Serve the brownies cold.

Chocolate Fudge Brownies

Makes 16

125 g/4 oz butter
175 g/6 oz plain dark chocolate,
roughly chopped or broken
225 g/8 oz caster sugar
2 tsp vanilla essence
2 medium eggs,
lightly beaten
150 g/5 oz plain flour
175 g/6 oz icing sugar
2 tbsp cocoa powder
15 g/^{1}/$_2$ oz butter

Preheat the oven to 180°C/350°F/Gas Mark 4, 10 minutes before baking. Lightly oil and line a 20.5 cm/8 inch square cake tin with greaseproof or baking paper.

Slowly melt the butter and chocolate together in a heatproof bowl set over a sauce-pan of simmering water. Transfer the mixture to a large bowl.

Stir in the sugar and vanilla essence, then stir in the eggs. Sift over the flour and fold together well with a metal spoon or rubber spatula. Pour into the prepared tin.

Transfer to the preheated oven and bake for 30 minutes until just set. Remove the cooked mixture from the oven and leave to cool in the tin before turning it out on to a wire rack.

Sift the icing sugar and cocoa powder into a small bowl and make a well in the centre. Place the butter in the well then gradually add about 2 tablespoons of hot water. Mix to form a smooth spreadable icing.

Pour the icing over the cooked mixture. Allow the icing to set before cutting into squares. Serve the brownies when they are cold.

White Chocolate Blondies

Makes 15

75 g/3 oz unsalted butter
200 g/7 oz demerara sugar
2 large eggs, lightly beaten
1 tsp vanilla extract
2 tbsp milk
125 g/4 oz plain flour,
plus 1 tbsp
1 tsp baking powder
pinch salt
75 g/3 oz walnuts,
roughly chopped
125 g/4 oz white
chocolate drops
1 tbsp icing sugar

Preheat the oven to 190°C/375°F/Gas Mark 5, 10 minutes before baking. Oil and line a 28 x 18 x 2.5 cm/11 x 7 x 1 inch cake tin with nonstick baking parchment.

Place the butter and demerara sugar into a heavy-based saucepan and heat gently until the butter has melted and the sugar has started to dissolve. Remove from the heat and leave to cool.

Place the eggs, vanilla extract and milk in a large bowl and beat together. Stir in the butter and sugar mixture, then sift in the 125 g/4 oz of flour, the baking powder and salt. Gently stir the mixture twice.

Toss the walnuts and chocolate drops into the remaining 1 tablespoon of flour to coat. Add to the bowl and stir the ingredients together gently.

Spoon the mixture into the prepared tin and bake on the centre shelf of the preheated oven for 35 minutes, or until the top is firm and slightly crusty. Place the tin on a wire rack and leave to cool. When completely cold, remove the cake from the tin and lightly dust the top with icing sugar. Using a sharp knife, cut into 15 blondies, and serve.

Lemon-iced Ginger Squares

Makes 12

225 g/8 oz caster sugar
50 g/2 oz butter, melted
2 tbsp black treacle
2 medium egg whites,
lightly whisked
225 g/8 oz plain flour
1 tsp bicarbonate of soda
$^{1}/_{2}$ tsp ground cloves
1 tsp ground cinnamon
$^{1}/_{4}$ tsp ground ginger
pinch salt
225 ml/8 fl oz buttermilk
175 g/6 oz icing sugar
2–4 tbsp lemon juice

Preheat the oven to 200°C/400°F/Gas Mark 6, 15 minutes before baking. Lightly oil a 20.5 cm/8 inch square cake tin and sprinkle with a little flour.

Mix together the caster sugar, butter and treacle. Stir in the egg whites.

In a separate bowl, mix together the flour, bicarbonate of soda, cloves, cinnamon, ginger and salt. Stir the flour mixture and buttermilk alternately into the butter mixture until blended well.

Spoon into the prepared tin and bake in the preheated oven for 35 minutes, or until a skewer inserted into the centre of the cake comes out clean.

Remove from the oven and allow to cool for 5 minutes in the tin before turning out on to a wire rack over a large plate. Using a cocktail stick, make holes on the top of the cake.

Meanwhile, mix together the icing sugar with enough lemon juice to make a smooth pourable icing. Carefully pour the icing over the hot cake, then leave until cold. Cut the ginger cake into squares and serve.

Apricot Almond Slice

Cuts into 10 slices

2 tbsp demerara sugar

25 g/1 oz flaked almonds

400 g can apricot halves, drained

225 g/8 oz butter

225 g/8 oz caster sugar

4 medium eggs

200 g/7 oz self-raising flour

25 g/1 oz ground almonds

$^1/_2$ tsp almond essence

50 g/2 oz ready-to-eat dried apricots, chopped

3 tbsp clear honey

3 tbsp roughly chopped almonds, toasted

Preheat the oven to 180°C/350°F/Gas Mark 4. Oil a 20.5 cm/8 inch square tin and line with non-stick baking paper.

Sprinkle the sugar and the flaked almonds over the paper, then arrange the apricot halves cut-side down on top.

Cream the butter and sugar together in a large bowl until light and fluffy. Gradually beat the eggs into the butter mixture, adding a spoonful of flour after each addition of egg.

When all the eggs have been added, stir in the remaining flour and ground almonds and mix thoroughly. Add the almond essence and the apricots and stir well.

Spoon the mixture into the prepared tin, taking care not to dislodge the apricot halves. Bake in the preheated oven for 1 hour, or until golden and firm to touch.

Remove from the oven and allow to cool slightly for 15–20 minutes. Turn out carefully, discard the lining paper and transfer to a serving dish. Pour the honey over the top of the cake, sprinkle on the toasted almonds and serve.

Citrus Chocolate Slices

Makes 12 slices

175 g/6 oz butter
175 g/6 oz soft light brown sugar
finely grated zest of 1 orange
3 medium eggs, lightly beaten
1 tbsp ground almonds
175 g/6 oz self-raising flour
$1/4$ tsp baking powder
125 g/4 oz dark chocolate,
coarsely grated
2 tsp milk

For the crunchy topping

125 g/4 oz granulated sugar
juice of 2 limes
juice of 1 orange

Preheat the oven to 170°C/325°F/Gas Mark 3, 10 minutes before baking. Oil and line a 28 x 18 x 2.5 cm/11 x 7 x 1 inch cake tin with nonstick baking parchment. Place the butter, sugar and orange zest into a large bowl and cream together until light and fluffy. Gradually add the eggs, beating after each addition, then beat in the ground almonds.

Sift the flour and baking powder into the creamed mixture. Add the grated chocolate and milk, then gently fold in using a metal spoon. Spoon the mixture into the prepared tin.

Bake on the centre shelf of the preheated oven for 35–40 minutes until well risen and firm to the touch. Leave in the tin for a few minutes to cool slightly. Turn out onto a wire rack and remove the baking parchment.

Meanwhile, make the crunchy topping. Place the sugar with the lime and orange juices into a small jug and stir together. Drizzle the sugar mixture over the hot cake, ensuring the whole surface is covered. Leave until completely cold, then cut into 12 slices and serve.

Lemon Bars

Makes 24

175 g/6 oz plain flour
125 g/4 oz butter
50 g/2 oz granulated sugar
200 g/7 oz caster sugar
2 tbsp plain flour
$^1/_2$ tsp baking powder
$^1/_4$ tsp salt
2 medium eggs,
lightly beaten
juice and finely grated
rind of 1 lemon
sifted icing sugar, to decorate

Preheat the oven to 170°C/325°F/Gas Mark 3, 10 minutes before baking. Lightly oil and line a 20.5 cm/8 inch square cake tin with greaseproof or baking paper.

Rub together the flour and butter until the mixture resembles breadcrumbs. Stir in the granulated sugar and mix.

Turn the mixture into the prepared tin and press down firmly. Bake in the preheated oven for 20 minutes, until pale golden.

Meanwhile, in a food processor, mix together the caster sugar, flour, baking powder, salt, eggs, lemon juice and rind until smooth. Pour over the prepared base.

Transfer to the preheated oven and bake for a further 20–25 minutes, until nearly set but still a bit wobbly in the centre. Remove from the oven and cool in the tin on a wire rack.

Dust with icing sugar and cut into squares. Serve cold or store in an airtight tin.

Apple Cinnamon Crumble Bars

Makes 16

450 g/1 lb Bramley cooking
apples, roughly chopped
50 g/2 oz raisins
50 g/2 oz caster sugar
1 tsp ground cinnamon
zest of 1 lemon
200 g/7 oz plain flour
250 g/9 oz soft light
brown sugar
½ tsp bicarbonate of soda
150 g/5 oz rolled oats
150 g/5 oz butter, melted
crème fraîche or whipped cream,
to serve

Preheat the oven to 190°C/375°F/Gas Mark 5, 10 minutes before baking. Place the apples, raisins, sugar, cinnamon and lemon zest into a saucepan over a low heat.

Cover and cook for about 15 minutes, stirring occasionally, until the apple is cooked through. Remove the cover and stir well with a wooden spoon to break up the apple completely.

Cook for a further 15–30 minutes over a very low heat until reduced, thickened and slightly darkened. Allow to cool. Lightly oil and line a 20.5 cm/8 inch square cake tin with greaseproof or baking paper.

Mix together the flour, sugar, bicarbonate of soda, rolled oats and butter until combined well and crumbly. Spread half of the flour mixture into the bottom of the prepared tin and press down. Pour over the apple mixture.

Sprinkle over the remaining flour mixture and press down lightly. Bake in the preheated oven for 30–35 minutes, until golden brown.

Remove from the oven and allow to cool before cutting into slices. Serve the bars warm or cold with crème fraîche or whipped cream.

Pecan Caramel Shortbread

Makes 20

125 g/4 oz butter, softened
2 tbsp smooth peanut butter
75 g/3 oz caster sugar
75 g/3 oz cornflour
175 g/6 oz plain flour

For the filling

200 g/7 oz caster sugar
125 g/4 oz butter
2 tbsp golden syrup
75 g/3 oz liquid glucose
85 ml/3 fl oz water
400 g can sweetened
condensed milk
175 g/6 oz pecans,
roughly chopped

For the topping

75 g/3 oz dark chocolate
1 tbsp butter

Preheat the oven to 180°C/350°F/Gas Mark 4, 10 minutes before baking. Lightly oil and line an 18 cm x 28 cm/7 x 11 inch tin with greaseproof paper.

Cream together the butter, peanut butter and sugar until light. Sift in the cornflour and flour together and mix in to make a smooth dough. Press the mixture into the tin and prick all over with a fork. Bake in the oven for 20 minutes, or until just golden. Remove from the oven.

Meanwhile, for the filling, place the sugar, butter, golden syrup, glucose, water and milk in a heavy-based saucepan. Stir constantly over a low heat without boiling, until the sugar has dissolved. Increase the heat and boil steadily, stirring constantly, for about 10 minutes until the mixture turns a golden caramel colour. Remove the saucepan from the heat and add the pecans. Pour over the shortbread base immediately. Allow to cool, then refrigerate for at least 1 hour.

Break the chocolate into small pieces and put into a heatproof bowl with the butter. Place over a saucepan of gently simmering water, ensuring that the bowl does not come into contact with the water. Leave until melted, then stir together well. Pour the chocolate evenly over the shortbread, spreading thinly to cover. Leave to set, cut into squares and serve.

Marbled Toffee Shortbread

Makes 12

175 g/6 oz butter
75 g/3 oz caster sugar
175 g/6 oz plain flour
25 g/1 oz cocoa powder
75 g/3 oz fine semolina

For the toffee filling:

50 g/2 oz butter
50 g/2 oz soft light
brown sugar

For the chocolate topping:

397 g can condensed milk
75 g/3 oz plain dark chocolate
75 g/3 oz milk chocolate
75 g/3 oz white chocolate

Preheat the oven to 180°C/350°F/Gas Mark 4, 10 minutes before baking. Oil and line a 20.5 cm /8 inch square cake tin with nonstick baking parchment. Cream the butter and sugar until light and fluffy then sift in the flour and cocoa powder. Add the semolina and mix together to form a soft dough. Press into the base of the prepared tin. Prick all over with a fork, then bake in the preheated oven for 25 minutes. Leave to cool.

To make the toffee filling, gently heat the butter, sugar and condensed milk together until the sugar has dissolved. Bring to the boil, then simmer for 5 minutes, stirring constantly. Leave for 1 minute, then spread over the shortbread and leave to cool.

For the topping, place the different chocolates in separate heatproof bowls and melt one at a time, set over a saucepan of almost boiling water. Drop spoonfuls of each on top of the toffee and tilt the tin to cover evenly. Swirl with a knife for a marbled effect.

Leave the chocolate to cool. When just set mark into fingers using a sharp knife. Leave for at least 1 hour to harden before cutting into fingers.

Fruit Nut Refrigerator Fingers

Makes 12

14 pink and white marshmallows
75 g/3 oz luxury dried mixed fruit
25 g/1 oz candied orange
peel, chopped
75 g/3 oz glacé cherries,
quartered
75 g/3 oz walnuts, chopped
1 tbsp brandy
175 g/6 oz digestive
biscuits, crushed
225 g/8 oz plain dark chocolate
125 g/4 oz unsalted butter
1 tbsp icing sugar, for
dusting, optional

Lightly oil and line the base of a 18 cm/7 inch tin with nonstick baking parchment. Using oiled kitchen scissors, snip each marshmallow into 4 or 5 pieces over a bowl. Add the dried mixed fruit, orange peel, cherries and walnuts to the bowl. Sprinkle with the brandy and stir together. Add the crushed biscuits and stir until mixed.

Break the chocolate into squares and put in a heatproof bowl with the butter set over a saucepan of almost boiling water. Stir occasionally until melted, then remove from the heat. Pour the melted chocolate mixture over the dry ingredients and mix together well. Spoon into the prepared tin, pressing down firmly.

Chill in the refrigerator for 15 minutes, then mark into 12 fingers using a sharp knife. Chill in the refrigerator for a further 1 hour or until set. Turn out of the tin, remove the lining paper and cut into fingers. Dust with icing sugar before serving.

All-in-one Chocolate Fudge Cakes

Makes 15 squares

175 g/6 oz soft dark
brown sugar
175 g/6 oz butter, softened
150 g/5 oz self-raising flour
25 g/1 oz cocoa powder
1/2 tsp baking powder
pinch salt
3 medium eggs,
lightly beaten
1 tbsp golden syrup

For the fudge topping:

75 g/3 oz granulated sugar
150 ml/¼ pint evaporated milk
175 g/6 oz plain dark chocolate,
roughly chopped
40 g/1½ oz unsalted
butter, softened
125 g/4 oz soft fudge
sweets, finely chopped

Preheat the oven to 180°C/350°F/Gas Mark 4, 10 minutes before baking. Oil and line a 28 x 18 x 2.5 cm/ 11 x 7 x 1 inch cake tin with non-stick baking parchment.

Place the soft brown sugar and butter in a bowl and sift in the flour, cocoa powder, baking powder and salt. Add the eggs and golden syrup, then beat with an electric whisk for 2 minutes, before adding 2 tablespoons of warm water and beating for a further 1 minute.

Turn the mixture into the prepared tin and level the top with the back of a spoon. Bake on the centre shelf of the preheated oven for 30 minutes, or until firm to the touch. Turn the cake out onto a wire rack and leave to cool before removing the baking parchment.

To make the topping, gently heat the sugar and evaporated milk in a saucepan, stirring frequently, until the sugar has dissolved. Bring the mixture to the boil and simmer for 6 minutes, without stirring.

Remove the mixture from the heat. Add the chocolate and butter and stir until melted and blended. Pour into a bowl and chill in the refrigerator for 1–2 hours or until thickened. Spread the topping over the cake, then sprinkle with the chopped fudge. Cut the cake into 15 squares before serving.

Marbled Chocolate Traybake

Makes 18 squares

175 g/6 oz butter
175 g/6 oz caster sugar
1 tsp vanilla extract
3 medium eggs,
lightly beaten
200 g/7 oz self-raising flour
$^1/_2$ tsp baking powder
1 tbsp milk
1 $^1/_2$ tbsp cocoa powder

For the chocolate icing

75 g/3 oz dark chocolate,
broken into pieces
75 g/3 oz white chocolate,
broken into pieces

Preheat the oven to 180°C/350°F/Gas Mark 4, 10 minutes before baking. Oil and line a 28 x 18 x 2.5 cm/11 x 7 x 1 inch cake tin with nonstick baking parchment.

Cream the butter, sugar and vanilla extract until light and fluffy. Gradually add the eggs, beating well after each addition. Sift in the flour and baking powder and fold in with the milk.

Spoon half the mixture into the prepared tin, spacing the spoonfuls apart, leaving gaps in between for the chocolate mixture. Blend the cocoa powder to a smooth paste with 2 tablespoons warm water. Stir this into the remaining cake mixture. Drop small spoonfuls between the vanilla cake mixture to fill in all the gaps. Use a knife to swirl the mixtures together a little.

Bake on the centre shelf of the preheated oven for 35 minutes, or until well risen and firm to the touch. Leave in the tin for 5 minutes to cool, then turn out onto a wire rack and leave to cool. Remove the parchment.

For the icing, place the dark and white chocolate in separate heatproof bowls and melt each over a saucepan of gently simmering water. Spoon into separate nonstick baking parchment piping bags, snip off the tips and drizzle over the top. Leave to set before cutting into squares.

Fig Chocolate Bars

Makes 12

125 g/4 oz butter
150 g/5 oz plain flour
50 g/2 oz soft light
brown sugar
225 g/8 oz ready-to-eat
dried figs, halved
juice of ¹/₂ a large lemon
1 tsp ground cinnamon
125 g/4 oz dark chocolate

Preheat the oven to 180°C/350°F/Gas Mark 4, 10 minutes before baking. Lightly oil an 18 cm/7 inch, square cake tin. Place the butter and the flour in a large bowl and, using your fingertips, rub the butter into the flour until it resembles fine breadcrumbs.

Stir in the sugar, then, using your hands, bring the mixture together to form a smooth dough. Knead until smooth, then press the dough into the prepared tin. Lightly prick the base with a fork and bake in the preheated oven for 20–30 minutes until golden. Remove from the oven and leave the shortbread to cool in the tin until completely cold.

Meanwhile, place the dried figs, lemon juice, 125 ml/4 fl oz water and the ground cinnamon in a saucepan and bring to the boil. Cover and simmer for 20 minutes, or until soft, stirring occasionally during cooking. Cool slightly, then purée in a food processor until smooth. Cool, then spread over the cooked shortbread.

Melt the chocolate in a heatproof bowl set over a saucepan of simmering water. Alternatively, the chocolate can be melted in the microwave according to the manufacturer's instructions. Stir until smooth, then spread over the top of the fig filling. Leave to become firm, then cut into 12 bars and serve.

Moist Mocha Coconut Cakes

Makes 9 squares

3 tbsp ground coffee
5 tbsp hot milk
75 g/3 oz butter
175 g/6 oz golden syrup
25 g/1 oz soft light brown sugar
40 g/1^1/$_2$ oz desiccated coconut
150 g/5 oz plain flour
25 g/1 oz cocoa powder
^{1}/$_2$ tsp bicarbonate of soda
2 medium eggs, lightly beaten
2 chocolate flakes, to decorate

For the coffee icing

225 g/8 oz icing sugar, sifted
125 g/4 oz butter, softened

Preheat the oven to 170˚C/ 325˚F/Gas Mark 3, 10 minutes before baking. Lightly oil and line a deep 20.5 cm/8 inch square tin with nonstick baking parchment. Place the ground coffee in a small bowl and pour over the hot milk. Leave to infuse for 5 minutes, then strain through a tea-strainer or a sieve lined with muslin. You will end up with about 4 tablespoons of liquid. Reserve.

Put the butter, golden syrup, sugar and coconut in a small heavy-based saucepan and heat gently until the butter has melted and the sugar dissolved. Sift the flour, cocoa powder and bicarbonate of soda together and stir into the melted mixture with the eggs and 3 tablespoons of the coffee-infused milk.

Pour the mixture into the prepared tin. Bake on the centre shelf of the preheated oven for 45 minutes, or until the cake is well risen and firm to the touch. Leave in the tin for 10 minutes to cool slightly, then turn out onto a wire rack to cool completely.

For the icing, gradually add the icing sugar to the butter and beat together until mixed. Add the remaining 1 tablespoon of coffee-infused milk and beat until light and fluffy. Carefully spread over the top of the cake, then cut into 9 squares. Decorate each with a small piece of chocolate flake and serve.

Classic Flapjacks

Makes 12

175 g/6 oz butter, plus extra
for greasing
125 g/4 oz demerara sugar
2 tbsp golden syrup
175 g/6 oz jumbo
porridge oats
few drops vanilla extract

Preheat the oven to 160°C/325°F/Gas Mark 3. Butter a 20.5 cm/8 inch square baking tin.

Place the butter, sugar and golden syrup in a saucepan and heat gently until the butter has melted and every grain of sugar has dissolved.

Remove from the heat and stir in the oats and vanilla extract. Stir well and then spoon the mixture into the prepared tin.

Smooth level with the back of a large spoon. Bake in the centre of the oven for 30–40 minutes until golden. Leave to cool in the tin for 10 minutes, then mark into fingers and leave in the tin until completely cold. When cold, cut into fingers with a sharp knife.

Fruit Nut Flapjacks

Makes 12

75 g/3 oz butter
or margarine
125 g/4 oz soft light
brown sugar
3 tbsp golden syrup
50 g/2 oz raisins
50 g/2 oz walnuts,
roughly chopped
175 g/6 oz rolled oats
50 g/2 oz icing sugar
1–1¹/₂ tbsp lemon juice

Preheat the oven to 180°C/350°F/Gas Mark 4, 10 minutes before baking. Lightly oil a 23 cm/9 inch square cake tin.

Melt the butter or margarine with the sugar and syrup in a small saucepan over a low heat. Remove from the heat. Stir the raisins, walnuts and oats into the syrup mixture and mix together well.

Spoon evenly into the prepared tin and press down well. Transfer to the preheated oven and bake for 20–25 minutes.

Remove from the oven and leave to cool in the tin. Cut into bars while still warm.

Sift the icing sugar into a small bowl then gradually beat in the lemon juice a little at a time to form a thin icing.

Place into an icing bag fitted with a writing nozzle then pipe thin lines over the flapjacks. Allow to cool and serve.

Chocolate-covered Flapjack

Makes 24

215 g/7½ oz plain flour
150 g/5 oz rolled oats
225 g/8 oz light muscovado sugar
1 tsp bicarbonate of soda
.pinch salt
150 g/5 oz butter
2 tbsp golden syrup
250 g/9 oz plain dark chocolate
5 tbsp double cream

Preheat the oven to 180°C/ 350°F/Gas Mark 4, 10 minutes before baking. Lightly oil a 33 x 23 cm/13 x 9 inch Swiss roll tin and line with nonstick baking parchment. Place the flour, rolled oats, the light muscovado sugar, bicarbonate of soda and salt into a bowl and stir well together.

Melt the butter and golden syrup together in a heavy-based saucepan and stir until smooth, then add to the oat mixture and mix together thoroughly. Spoon the mixture into the prepared tin and press down firmly and level the top.

Bake in the preheated oven for 15–20 minutes or until golden. Remove from the oven and leave the flapjack to cool in the tin. Once cool, remove from the tin. Discard the parchment.

Melt the chocolate in a heatproof bowl set over a saucepan of gently simmering water. Alternatively, melt the chocolate in the microwave according to the manufacturer's instructions. Once the chocolate has melted quickly beat in the cream, then pour over the flapjack. Mark patterns over the chocolate with a fork when almost set.

Chill the flapjack in the refrigerator for at least 30 minutes before cutting into bars. When the chocolate has set, serve. Store in an airtight container for a few days.

Chocolate Pecan Traybake

Makes 12

175 g/6 oz butter
75 g/3 oz icing sugar, sifted
175 g/6 oz plain flour
25 g/1 oz self-raising flour
25 g/1 oz cocoa powder

For the pecan topping

75 g/3 oz butter
50 g/2 oz light
muscovado sugar
2 tbsp golden syrup
2 tbsp milk
1 tsp vanilla extract
2 medium eggs,
lightly beaten
125 g/4 oz pecan halves

Preheat the oven to 180°C/350°F/Gas Mark 4, 10 minutes before baking. Lightly oil and line a 28 x 18 x 2.5 cm/11 x 7 x 1 inch cake tin with nonstick baking parchment.

Beat the butter and sugar together until light and fluffy. Sift in the flours and cocoa powder and mix together to form a soft dough.

Press the mixture evenly over the base of the prepared tin. Prick all over with a fork, then bake on the shelf above the centre of the preheated oven for 15 minutes.

Put the butter, sugar, golden syrup, milk and vanilla extract in a small saucepan and heat gently until melted. Remove from the heat and leave to cool for a few minutes, then stir in the eggs and pour over the base. Sprinkle with the nuts.

Bake in the preheated oven for 25 minutes, or until dark golden brown, but still slightly soft. Leave to cool in the tin. When cool, carefully remove from the tin, then cut into 12 squares and serve. Store in an airtight container.

Miracle Bars

Makes 12

100 g/3½ oz butter, melted,
plus 1–2 tsp extra
for greasing
125 g/4 oz digestive
biscuit crumbs
175 g/6 oz chocolate chips
75 g/3 oz shredded or
desiccated coconut
125 g/4 oz chopped
mixed nuts
400 g can sweetened
condensed milk

Preheat the oven to 180°C/350°F/Gas Mark 4, 10 minutes before baking. Generously grease a 23 cm/9 inch, square tin and line with nonstick baking paper.

Pour the butter into the prepared tin and sprinkle the biscuit crumbs over in an even layer. Add the chocolate chips, coconut and nuts in even layers and drizzle over the condensed milk.

Transfer the tin to the preheated oven and bake for 30 minutes until golden brown. Allow to cool in the tin, then cut into 12 squares and serve.

Nanaimo Bars

Makes 15

75 g/3 oz unsalted butter
125 g/4 oz dark chocolate,
roughly chopped
75 g/3 oz digestive
biscuits, crushed
75 g/3 oz desiccated coconut
50 g/2 oz chopped mixed nuts

For the filling

1 medium egg yolk
1 tbsp milk
75 g/3 oz unsalted
butter, softened
1 tsp vanilla extract
150 g/5 oz icing sugar

For the topping

125 g/4 oz dark
chocolate, chopped
2 tsp sunflower oil

Oil and line a 28 x 18 x 2.5 cm/11 x 7 x 1 inch cake tin with nonstick baking parchment. Place the butter and chocolate in a heatproof bowl set over a saucepan of gently simmering water until melted, stirring occasionally. Stir in the crushed biscuits, coconut and nuts into the chocolate mixture and mix well. Spoon into the prepared tin and press down firmly. Chill in the refrigerator for 20 minutes.

For the filling, place the egg yolk and milk in a heatproof bowl set over a saucepan of gently simmering water, making sure the bowl does not touch the water. Whisk for 2–3 minutes. Add the butter and vanilla extract to the bowl and continue whisking until fluffy, then gradually whisk in the icing sugar. Spread over the chilled base, smoothing with the back of a spoon, and chill in the refrigerator for a further 30 minutes.

For the topping, place the chocolate and sunflower oil in a heatproof bowl set over a saucepan of gently simmering water. Melt, stirring occasionally, until smooth. Leave to cool slightly, then pour over the filling and tilt the tin so that the chocolate spreads evenly.

Chill in the refrigerator for about 5 minutes until the chocolate topping is just set but not too hard, then mark into 15 bars. Chill again in the refrigerator for 2 hours, then cut into slices and serve.

Moist Mincemeat Tea Loaf

Cuts into 12 slices

225 g/8 oz self-raising flour
¹/₂ tsp ground mixed spice
125 g/4 oz cold butter, cubed
75 g/3 oz flaked almonds
25 g/1 oz glacé cherries, rinsed, dried and quartered
75 g/3 oz light muscovado sugar
2 medium eggs
250 g/9 oz prepared mincemeat
1 tsp lemon zest
2 tsp brandy or milk

Preheat the oven to 180°C/350°F/Gas Mark 4, 10 minutes before baking. Oil and line the base of a 900 g/2 lb loaf tin with nonstick baking paper.

Sift the flour and mixed spice into a large bowl. Add the butter and rub in until the mixture resembles breadcrumbs.

Reserve 2 tablespoons of the flaked almonds and stir in the rest with the glacé cherries and sugar. Make a well in the centre of the dry ingredients. Lightly whisk the eggs, then stir in the mincemeat, lemon zest and brandy or milk. Add the egg mixture and fold together until blended. Spoon into the prepared loaf tin, smooth the top with the back of a spoon, then sprinkle over the reserved flaked almonds.

Bake on the centre shelf of the oven for 30 minutes. Cover with foil to prevent the almonds browning too much. Bake for a further 30 minutes, or until risen and a skewer inserted into the centre comes out clean.

Leave the tea loaf in the tin for 10 minutes before removing and cooling on a wire rack. Remove the lining paper, slice thickly and serve.

Butterscotch Loaf

Serves 8

1 banana, peeled, weighing about
100 g/3¹/₂ oz
125 g/4 oz soft margarine
125 g/4 oz golden
caster sugar
2 medium eggs
1 tsp almond extract
¹/₂ tsp vanilla extract
125 g/4 oz self-raising flour
75 g/3 oz dark
chocolate chips
75 g/3 oz walnuts, chopped

To decorate:

50 g/2 oz natural icing sugar
25 g/1 oz golden lump sugar

Preheat the oven to 170°C/325°F/Gas Mark 3. Grease and line the base of a 1 kg/2 lb 3 oz loaf tin with a long thin strip of nonstick baking parchment.

Place the banana in a bowl and mash. Add the margarine, sugar and eggs along with the extracts and sift in the flour. Beat until smooth, then stir in the chocolate chips and add half the chopped walnuts. Stir until smooth, then spoon into the tin and spread level.

Bake for about 45 minutes until a skewer inserted into the centre comes out clean. Leave in the tin for 5 minutes, then turn out to cool on a wire rack, peel away the paper and leave to cool.

To decorate, make the icing sugar into a runny consistency with 2 teaspoons water. Drizzle over the cake and sprinkle over the remaining walnuts and the sugar lumps. Leave to set for 30 minutes, then serve sliced.

Fruity Apple Tea Bread

Cuts into 12 slices

125 g/4 oz butter
125 g/4 oz soft light brown sugar
275 g/10 oz sultanas
150 ml/¼ pint apple juice
1 eating apple, peeled, cored and chopped
2 medium eggs, beaten
275 g/10 oz plain flour
½ tsp ground cinnamon
½ tsp ground ginger
1 eating apple, cored and sliced
2 tsp bicarbonate of soda
1 tsp lemon juice

To decorate

1 tbsp golden syrup, warmed
curls of butter, to serve

Preheat the oven to 180°C/350°F/Gas Mark 4. Oil and line the base of a 900 g/2 lb loaf tin with nonstick baking paper.

Put the butter, sugar, sultanas and apple juice in a small saucepan. Heat gently, stirring occasionally, until the butter has melted. Tip into a bowl and leave to cool. Stir in the chopped apple and beaten eggs. Sift the flour, spices and bicarbonate of soda over the apple mixture and stir into the mixture. Spoon into the prepared loaf tin and smooth the top level with the back of a spoon.

Toss the apple slices in the lemon juice and arrange on top. Bake in the preheated oven for 50 minutes. Cover with foil to prevent the top from browning too much.

Bake for 30–35 minutes until a skewer inserted into the centre comes out clean.

Leave in the tin for 10 minutes before turning out to cool on a wire rack. Brush the top with golden syrup and leave to cool. Remove the lining paper, cut into thick slices and serve with curls of butter.

Marmalade Loaf Cake

Serves 8–10

175 g/6 oz natural golden
caster sugar
175 g/6 oz butter, softened
3 medium eggs, beaten
175 g/6 oz self-raising flour
finely grated zest and juice
of 1 orange
100 g/3¹/₂ oz orange marmalade

For the topping:

zest and juice of 1 orange
125 g/4 oz icing sugar

Preheat the oven to 180°C/350°F/Gas Mark 4. Grease and line a
1 kg/2 lb 3 oz loaf tin with a long thin strip of nonstick baking parchment.

Place the sugar and butter in a bowl and whisk until light and fluffy.
Add the beaten egg a little at a time, adding 1 teaspoon flour with
each addition.

Add the remaining flour to the bowl with the orange zest, 2 tablespoons
orange juice and the marmalade. Using a large metal spoon, fold the
mixture together using a figure-of-eight movement until all the flour is
incorporated. Spoon the batter into the tin and smooth level.

Bake for about 40 minutes until firm in the centre and a skewer inserted
into the centre comes out clean. Cool in the tin for 5 minutes, then turn
out to cool on a wire rack.

To make the topping, peel thin strips of zest away from the orange and
set aside. Squeeze the juice from the orange. Sift the icing sugar into
a bowl and mix with 1 tablespoon orange juice until a thin smooth
consistency forms. Drizzle over the top of the cake, letting it run down
the sides. Scatter over the orange zest and leave to set for 1 hour.

Maple, Pecan & Lemon Loaf

Cuts into 12 slices

350 g/12 oz plain flour
1 tsp baking powder
175 g/6 oz butter, cubed
75 g/3 oz caster sugar
125 g/4 oz pecan nuts,
roughly chopped
3 medium eggs
1 tbsp milk
finely grated zest of 1 lemon
5 tbsp maple syrup

For the icing

75 g/3 oz icing sugar
1 tbsp lemon juice
25 g/1 oz pecans,
roughly chopped

Preheat the oven to 170°C/325°F/Gas Mark 3, 10 minutes before baking. Lightly oil and line the base of a 900 g/2 lb loaf tin with nonstick baking parchment.

Sift the flour and baking powder into a large bowl. Rub in the butter until the mixture resembles fine breadcrumbs. Stir in the caster sugar and pecan nuts.

Beat the eggs together with the milk and lemon zest. Stir in the maple syrup. Add to the dry ingredients and gently stir in until mixed thoroughly to make a soft dropping consistency. Spoon the mixture into the prepared tin and level the top with the back of a spoon. Bake on the centre shelf of the preheated oven for 50–60 minutes until the cake is well risen and lightly browned. If a skewer inserted into the centre comes out clean, then the cake is ready. Leave the cake in the tin for about 10 minutes, then turn out and leave to cool on a wire rack. Carefully remove the lining paper.

Sift the icing sugar into a small bowl and stir in the lemon juice to make a smooth icing. Drizzle the icing over the top of the loaf, then scatter with the chopped pecans. Leave to set, slice thickly and serve.

Banana Honey Tea Bread

Makes one 900 g/2 lb loaf

2 large peeled bananas, about 225 g/8 oz
1 tbsp fresh orange juice
125 g/4 oz soft margarine
125 g/4 oz soft light brown sugar
125 g/4 oz honey
2 medium eggs, beaten
225 g/8 oz wholemeal self-raising flour
½ tsp ground cinnamon
75 g/3 oz sultanas

Preheat the oven to 180°C/350°F/Gas Mark 4. Grease a 900 g/2 lb loaf tin and line the base with a strip of nonstick baking parchment. Mash the bananas together in a large bowl with the orange juice.

Place the soft margarine, sugar and honey in the bowl and add the eggs. Sift in the flour and cinnamon, adding any bran left behind in the sieve. Beat everything together until light and fluffy and then fold in the sultanas.

Spoon the mixture into the prepared tin and smooth the top to make it level. Bake for about 1 hour until golden, well risen and a skewer inserted into the centre comes out clean.

Cool in the tin for 5 minutes, then turn out on a wire rack.

Small Cakes, Buns & Pastries

These tasty treats are the perfect accompaniment to a well-earned cup of tea or coffee, and also make great fresh alternatives to shop-bought lunchbox snacks. For a light and airy taste of France try the Chocolate Madeleines; or for an unusual twist, go for a batch of Rhubarb & Custard Muffins. There are also some pastries to jazz up breakfast time, from Easy Danish Pasties to Fruited Brioche Buns, yum!

Gingerbread Cupcakes

Makes 14–16

8 tbsp golden syrup
125 g/4 oz block margarine
225 g/8 oz plain flour
2 tsp ground ginger
75 g/3 oz sultanas
50 g/2 oz soft dark
brown sugar
175 ml/6 fl oz milk
1 tsp bicarbonate of soda
1 medium egg, beaten
125 g/4 oz golden icing sugar,
to decorate

Preheat the oven to 180°C/350°F/Gas Mark 4. Line one or two trays with 14–16 deep paper cases, depending on the size of the holes.

Place the syrup and margarine in a heavy-based pan and melt together gently. Sift the flour and ginger into a bowl, then stir in the sultanas and sugar.

Warm the milk and stir in the bicarbonate of soda. Pour the syrup mixture, the milk and the beaten egg into the dry ingredients and beat until smooth.

Spoon the mixture halfway up each case and bake for 25–30 minutes until risen and firm. Cool in the trays for 10 minutes, then turn out to cool on a wire rack.

To decorate the cupcakes, blend the icing sugar with 1 tablespoon warm water to make a thin glacé icing. Place in a paper icing bag and snip away the tip. Drizzle over the top of each cupcake in a lacy pattern. Keep in an airtight container for up to 5 days.

Lemon Drizzle Cupcakes

Makes 12 deep cupcakes or 18 fairy cakes

150 g/5 oz butter, softened
150 g/5 oz caster sugar
3 medium eggs, beaten
150 g/5 oz self-raising flour
$^1/_2$ tsp baking powder
1 lemon

To decorate

1 lemon
50 g/2 oz caster sugar

Preheat the oven to 180°C/350°F/Gas Mark 4 and line a 12-hole tray with paper cases, or two fairy-cake trays with 18 fairy-cake cases.

Place the butter, sugar and eggs in a bowl and then sift in the flour and baking powder. Finely grate the zest of the lemon into the bowl.

Beat together for about 2 minutes, preferably with an electric hand-mixer, until pale and fluffy. Spoon into the paper cases and bake for 25 minutes for the larger cupcakes and 15 minutes for the fairy cakes until firm and golden. Cool on a wire rack.

To make the topping, cut the zest from the other lemon into thin strips and set aside. Squeeze the juice from the lemon into a small saucepan. Add the sugar and heat gently until every grain of sugar has dissolved.

Add the strips of zest and cool slightly. Spoon the syrup and lemon strips over the cupcakes while still warm. Leave to cool. Keep for 4 days in an airtight container.

Cappuccino Cakes

Makes 6

125 g/4 oz butter or margarine
125 g/4 oz caster sugar
2 medium eggs
1 tbsp strong black coffee
150 g/5 oz self-raising flour
125 g/4 oz mascarpone cheese
1 tbsp icing sugar, sifted
1 tsp vanilla extract
sifted cocoa powder, for dusting

Preheat the oven to 190°C/375°F/Gas Mark 5, 10 minutes before baking. Place six large paper muffin cases into a muffin tray, or place onto a baking sheet.

Cream the butter or margarine and sugar together until light and fluffy. Break the eggs into a small bowl and beat lightly with a fork. Using a wooden spoon, beat the eggs into the butter and sugar mixture a little at a time, until they are all incorporated. If the mixture looks curdled, beat in a spoonful of the flour to return the mixture to a smooth consistency. Finally, beat in the black coffee.

Sift the flour into the mixture, then, with a metal spoon or rubber spatula, gently fold in the flour. Place spoonfuls of the mixture into the muffin cases.

Bake in the preheated oven for 20–25 minutes, until risen and springy to the touch. Cool on a wire rack.

In a small bowl, beat together the mascarpone cheese, icing sugar and vanilla extract. When the cakes are cold, spoon the vanilla mascarpone onto the top of each one. Dust with cocoa powder and serve. Eat within 24 hours and store in the refrigerator.

Lemon Cardamom Cupcakes

Makes 12

1 tsp cardamom pods
200 g/7 oz butter
50 g/2 oz plain flour
200 g/7 oz self-raising flour
1 tsp baking powder
200 g/7 oz caster sugar
zest of 1 lemon, finely grated
3 medium eggs
100 ml/3¹/₂ fl oz natural yogurt
4 tbsp lemon curd

To decorate

250 g/9 oz tub mascarpone
6 tbsp icing sugar
1 tsp lemon juice lemon zest strips

Preheat the oven to 180°C/350°F/Gas Mark 4. Line a 12-hole tray with deep paper cases. Crush the cardamom pods and remove the outer cases. Melt the butter and leave aside to cool.

Sift the flours and baking powder into a bowl and stir in the crushed seeds, sugar and lemon zest. In another bowl, whisk together the eggs and yogurt. Pour into the dry ingredients with the cooled melted butter and beat until combined.

Divide half the mixture between the paper cases, put a teaspoon of lemon curd into each, then top with the remaining mixture. Bake for about 25 minutes until golden.

To make the topping, beat the mascarpone with the icing sugar and lemon juice. Swirl onto each cupcake and top with lemon strips. Eat fresh on the day of baking once decorated, or store, undecorated, in an airtight container for up to 2 days and add the topping just before serving.

Honey Spice Cupcakes

Makes 12–14

1 tsp instant coffee granules
6 tbsp hot water
175 g/6 oz plain flour
1 tsp baking powder
$^1/_2$ tsp bicarbonate of soda
$^1/_2$ tsp ground cinnamon
$^1/_2$ tsp ground ginger
pinch ground cloves
2 medium eggs
125 g/4 oz golden caster sugar
175 g/6 oz honey
5 tbsp vegetable oil
50 g/2 oz walnuts, finely chopped
125 g/4 oz golden icing
sugar, to decorate

Preheat the oven to 160°C/325°F/Gas Mark 3. Line one or two trays with 12–14 deep paper cases, depending on the depth of the holes. Dissolve the coffee in the water and leave aside to cool.

Sift the flour with the baking powder, bicarbonate of soda and spices. In another bowl, beat the eggs with the sugar and honey until smooth and light, then gradually beat in the oil until blended. Stir this into the flour mixture along with the coffee and walnuts. Beat until smooth.

Carefully spoon the mixture into the paper cases. Fill each halfway up. Take care not to overfill them, as the mixture will rise up. Bake for 25–30 minutes until they are risen, firm and golden. Leave in the trays for 5 minutes, then turn out onto a wire rack to cool.

To decorate, blend the icing sugar with 1 tablespoon warm water to make a thin glacé icing. Place in a paper icing bag and snip away the tip. Pipe large daisies round the sides of each cupcake and leave to set for 30 minutes. Keep in an airtight container for up to 5 days.

Mini Carrot Cupcakes

Makes 22

175 g/6 oz self-raising
wholemeal flour
1 tsp baking powder
1/2 tsp ground cinnamon
pinch salt
150 ml/1/4 pint sunflower oil
150 g/5 oz soft light brown sugar
3 medium eggs, beaten
1 tsp vanilla extract
50 g/2 oz sultanas
225 g/8 oz carrots, peeled
and grated

To decorate

1 orange
75 g/3 oz cream cheese
175 g/6 oz golden icing sugar

Preheat the oven to 180°C/350°F/Gas Mark 4. Lightly oil two 12-hole mini trays.

Sift the flour, baking powder, cinnamon and salt into a bowl, along with any bran from the sieve. Add the oil, sugar, eggs, vanilla extract, sultanas and grated carrots.

Beat until smooth, then spoon into the trays. Bake for about 20 minutes until risen and golden. Cool on a wire rack.

To decorate, peel thin strips of zest from the orange. Beat the cream cheese and icing sugar together with 2 teaspoons juice from the orange to make a spreading consistency. Swirl the icing over each cupcake and then top with shreds of orange zest. Keep for 3 days in an airtight container in a cool place.

Fudgy Top Hat Chocolate Buns

Makes 12

50 g/2 oz self-raising flour
25 g/1 oz cocoa powder
1/2 tsp baking powder
75 g/3 oz butter, softened
75 g/3 oz soft light brown sugar
1 medium egg, lightly beaten
1 tbsp milk

For the fudgy icing

15 g/1/2 oz unsalted butter, melted
1 tbsp milk
15 g/1/2 oz cocoa powder, sifted
40 g/11/2 oz icing sugar, sifted
25 g/1 oz dark chocolate,
coarsely grated

For the top hat filling

150 ml/1/4 pint whipping cream
2 tsp orange liqueur
1 tbsp icing sugar, sifted

Preheat the oven to 190°C/375°F/Gas Mark 5, 10 minutes before baking. Sift the flour, cocoa powder and baking powder into a bowl. Add the butter, sugar, egg and milk. Beat for 2–3 minutes until light and fluffy. Divide the mixture equally between 12 paper cases arranged in a bun tray. Bake on the shelf above the centre in the preheated oven for 15–20 minutes until well risen and firm to the touch. Leave in the bun tray for a few minutes, then transfer to a wire rack and leave to cool completely.

For the fudgy icing, mix together the melted butter, milk, cocoa powder and icing sugar. Place a spoonful of icing on the top of 6 of the buns, spreading out to a circle with the back of the spoon. Sprinkle with grated chocolate. To make the top hats, use a sharp knife to cut and remove a circle of sponge, about 3 cm/11/2 inches across, from each of the 6 remaining cakes. Whip the cream, orange liqueur and the icing sugar together until soft peaks form.

Spoon the filling into a piping bag fitted with a large star nozzle and pipe a swirl in the centre of each cake. Replace the tops, then dust with the remaining icing sugar and serve with the other buns.

Double Chocolate Chip Cupcakes

Makes 14

125 g/4 oz soft margarine
125 g/4 oz golden caster sugar
2 medium eggs, beaten
25 g/1 oz cocoa powder
175 g/6 oz self-raising flour
1 tsp baking powder
50 g/2 oz milk chocolate chips
50 g/2 oz dark or white
chocolate chips
1 tbsp milk

Preheat the oven to 180°C/350°F/Gas Mark 4. Line one or two bun trays with 14 small paper cases.

Place the margarine and sugar in a large bowl with the eggs and sift in the cocoa powder, flour and baking powder. Beat for about 2 minutes until smooth, then fold in the chocolate chips with the milk.

Spoon into the paper cases and bake for 15–20 minutes until firm. Place on a wire rack to cool. Keep for 4–5 days in an airtight container.

Rich Chocolate Cupcakes

Makes 12

175 g/6 oz self-raising flour
25 g/1 oz cocoa powder
175 g/6 oz soft light brown sugar
75 g/3 oz butter, melted
2 medium eggs, lightly beaten
1 tsp vanilla extract
40 g/1 1/2 oz maraschino cherries,
drained and chopped

For the chocolate icing

50 g/2 oz dark chocolate
25 g/1 oz unsalted butter
25 g/1 oz icing sugar, sifted

For the cherry icing

125 g/4 oz icing sugar
10 g/1/4 oz unsalted butter, melted
1 tsp syrup from the
maraschino cherries
3 maraschino cherries,
halved, to decorate

Preheat the oven to 180°C/350°F/Gas Mark 4, 10 minutes before baking. Line a 12-hole muffin or deep bun tray with paper muffin cases.

Sift the flour and cocoa powder into a bowl. Stir in the sugar, then add the melted butter, eggs and vanilla extract. Beat together for 3 minutes, or until well blended. Divide half the mixture between six of the paper cases. Dry the cherries thoroughly on absorbent kitchen paper, then fold into the remaining mixture and spoon into the rest of the paper cases. Bake on the shelf above the centre of the oven for 20 minutes, or until a skewer inserted into the centre of a cake comes out clean. Transfer to a wire rack and leave to cool.

For the chocolate icing, melt the chocolate and butter in a heatproof bowl over a saucepan of simmering water. Remove from the heat and leave to cool for 3 minutes, stirring occasionally. Stir in the icing sugar. Spoon over the chocolate cakes and leave to set.

For the cherry icing, sift the icing sugar into a bowl and stir in 1 tablespoon boiling water, the butter and cherry syrup. Spoon the icing over the remaining six cakes, decorate with halved cherries and leave to set.

Chocolate Madeleines

Makes 10

125 g/4 oz butter
125 g/4 oz soft light
brown sugar
2 medium eggs, lightly beaten
1 drop almond extract
1 tbsp ground almonds
75 g/3 oz self-raising flour
20 g/³/₄ oz cocoa powder
1 tsp baking powder

To finish

5 tbsp apricot conserve
1 tbsp amaretto liqueur, brandy or
orange juice
50 g/2 oz desiccated coconut
10 large chocolate
buttons (optional)

Preheat the oven to 180°C/350°F/Gas Mark 4, 10 minutes before baking. Lightly oil 10 dariole moulds and line the base of each with a small circle of nonstick baking parchment. Stand the moulds on a baking tray.

Cream the butter and sugar together until light and fluffy. Gradually add the eggs, beating well after each addition. Beat in the almond extract and ground almonds. Sift the flour, cocoa powder and baking powder over the creamed mixture. Gently fold in using a metal spoon. Divide the mixture equally between the prepared moulds – each should be about half full.

Bake on the centre shelf of the oven for 20 minutes, or until well risen and firm to the touch. Leave in the moulds for a few minutes, then run a small palette knife round the edge and turn out onto a wire rack to cool. Remove the paper circles from the sponges.

Heat the conserve with the liqueur, brandy or juice in a small saucepan. Sieve to remove any lumps. If necessary, trim the sponge bases, so they are flat. Brush the tops and sides with warm conserve, then roll in the coconut. Top each with a chocolate button, if using, fixed by brushing its base with conserve.

Date, Orange Walnut Muffins

Makes 12

275 g/10 oz plain flour
1 tbsp baking powder
125 g/4 oz golden
caster sugar
175 g/6 oz stoned
dates, chopped
50 g/2 oz chopped walnuts
1 medium egg
200 ml/7 fl oz milk
finely grated zest and juice
of 1 orange
6 tbsp sunflower oil

Preheat the oven to 200°C/400°F/Gas Mark 6. Line a deep 12-hole muffin tray with deep paper cases.

Sift the flour and baking powder into a bowl and make a well in the centre.

Add all the remaining ingredients and beat together until just combined. Spoon the batter into the paper cases and bake for about 16–18 minutes until well risen and firm to the touch.

Serve warm or cold and eat the muffins on the day of baking.

Blueberry Buttermilk Muffins

Makes 6–8

175 g/6 oz plain flour
1 tsp baking powder
175 g/6 oz golden caster sugar
175 ml/6 fl oz buttermilk
1 medium egg
$^1/_2$ tsp vanilla extract
40 g/1$^1/_2$ oz butter, melted
and cooled
150 g/5 oz fresh blueberries

Preheat the oven to 180°C/350°F/Gas Mark 4. Line a deep muffin tray with 6–8 paper cases, depending on the depth of the holes.

Sift the flour and baking powder into a bowl, then add the sugar. In another bowl, beat the buttermilk with the egg and vanilla extract, then pour into the dry ingredients. Mix with a fork, then add the cooled melted butter and stir until mixed but still slightly lumpy.

Gently fold in the blueberries. Spoon the mixture into the muffin cases, filling each two-thirds full. Bake for about 20 minutes until springy in the centre. Leave in the trays for 5 minutes, then turn out onto a wire rack to finish cooling. Eat warm or cold on the day of baking.

Coconut Lime Muffins

Makes 12

125 g/4 oz soft margarine
125 g/4 oz golden
caster sugar
2 medium eggs
50 g/2 oz desiccated coconut
1 lime
125 g/4 oz self-raising flour
1 tsp baking powder
2 tbsp milk

To decorate:

40 g/1^1/$_2$ oz unsalted butter
125 g/4 oz icing sugar
50 g/2 oz coconut chips
zest of 1 lime, grated

Preheat the oven to 180°C/350°F/Gas Mark 4. Line a deep 12-hole muffin tray with deep paper cases.

Place the margarine and caster sugar in a bowl and add the eggs and coconut. Finely grate the zest from the lime into the bowl, then squeeze in the juice. Sift in the flour and baking powder.

Add the milk and whisk together for about 2 minutes with an electric beater, or by hand until smooth, then spoon into the paper cases. Bake for 15–20 minutes until golden and firm. Cool on a wire rack.

To decorate the muffins, beat the butter and icing sugar together until smooth, then pipe or swirl onto each muffin. Press the coconut chips into the buttercream and then scatter the grated lime zest on top. Keep for 3 days in an airtight container in a cool place.

Ginger Apricot Mini Muffins

Makes 18

75 g/3 oz plain flour
75 g/3 oz wholemeal flour
2 tsp baking powder
$^1/_2$ tsp ground cinnamon
50 g/2 oz soft light
brown sugar
1 medium egg
135 ml/4$^1/_2$ fl oz milk
75 g/3 oz butter, melted
125 g/4 oz canned
apricots, drained and
finely chopped
50 g/2 oz glacé ginger, chopped
50 g/2 oz chopped almonds
sparkly sugar pieces,
to decorate

Preheat the oven to 200°C/400°F/Gas Mark 6. Line one or two mini-muffin trays with 18 mini paper cases.

Sift the flours, baking powder and cinnamon into a bowl, adding any bran from the sieve, then stir in the sugar. In another bowl, beat the egg and milk together and then pour into the dry ingredients.

Add the melted butter, apricots, ginger and half the almonds and mix quickly with a fork until just combined.

Spoon the mixture into the cases. Scatter the other half of the almonds and the sugar crystals over the top. Bake for 15–20 minutes until risen and golden. Turn out onto a wire rack to cool and eat fresh on the day of baking.

Simnel Easter Muffins

Makes 6–8

125 g/4 oz yellow marzipan
150 ml/¹/₄ pint milk
50 g/2 oz soft light brown sugar
2 medium eggs
175 g/6 oz self-raising flour
¹/₂ tsp mixed spice
75 g/3 oz mixed dried fruit
50 g/2 oz glacé cherries, washed
and chopped
75 g/3 oz butter, melted
and cooled

Preheat the oven to 190°C/375°F/Gas Mark 5. Line a deep muffin tray with 6–8 paper cases, depending on the depth of the holes. Weigh 25 g/1 oz of the marzipan and roll into long thin strips. Grate or chop the remaining marzipan into small chunks.

Whisk the milk, sugar and eggs together in a jug. Sift the flour and spice into a bowl, then stir together with the fruit, cherries and the marzipan chunks. Pour the milk mixture into the flour mixture along with the melted butter. Mix until combined.

Spoon into the paper cases and make a cross over the top of each using two marzipan strips. Bake for about 20 minutes until firm in the centre. Cool in the tins for 3 minutes, then turn out to cool on a wire rack. Eat warm or cold. Keep for 24 hours sealed in an airtight container.

Fruity Buttermilk Muffins

Makes 12

175 g/6 oz self-raising flour
50 g/2 oz wholemeal
self-raising flour
1 tsp mixed ground spice
½ tsp bicarbonate of soda
1 medium egg
2 tbsp fine-cut orange
shred marmalade
125 ml/4 fl oz milk
50 ml/2 fl oz buttermilk
5 tbsp sunflower oil
125 g/4 oz eating apple, peeled,
cored and diced
125 g/4 oz ready-to-eat pitted
prunes, roughly chopped

Preheat the oven to 200°C/400°F/Gas Mark 6. Line a deep 12-hole muffin tray with deep paper cases.

Sift the flours, spice and bicarbonate of soda into a bowl. In another bowl, beat the egg with the marmalade, milk, buttermilk and oil and pour into the dry ingredients.

Stir with a fork until just combined, then fold in the apple and chopped prunes. Spoon into the cases and bake for about 20 minutes until golden, risen and firm to the touch.

Leave in the tins for 4 minutes, then turn out onto a wire rack to finish cooling. Serve warm or cold and eat on the day of baking.

Coffee Walnut Muffins

Makes 12

125 g/4 oz butter, softened
125 g/4 oz soft light
brown sugar
150 g/5 oz plain flour
1 tsp baking powder
2 medium eggs
1 tbsp golden syrup
1 tsp vanilla extract
4 tbsp sour cream
40 g/1½ oz walnut pieces,
chopped

To decorate:

150 ml/¼ pint double cream
1 tbsp golden caster sugar
1 tsp coffee extract
½ tsp ground cinnamon
50 g/2 oz walnut pieces

Preheat the oven to 180°C/350°F/Gas Mark 4. Grease or line a 12-hole muffin tray with paper cases.

Beat the butter and sugar together until light and fluffy. Sift in the flour and baking powder, then add the eggs, golden syrup, vanilla extract and soured cream. Beat together until fluffy, then fold in the nuts.

Spoon the batter into the paper cases, filling them about three-quarters full. Bake for about 25 minutes until a skewer inserted into the centre comes out clean. Turn out to cool on a wire rack.

For the topping, put the cream, sugar, coffee extract and cinnamon in a bowl and whisk until soft peaks form. Swirl over the muffins and top each with a walnut piece. Refrigerate until needed, or keep chilled for 24 hours in an airtight container.

Tropical Mango Muffins

Makes 10

50 g/2 oz soft dried
pineapple chunks
50 g/2 oz soft dried papaya pieces
25 g/1 oz soft dried mango pieces
225 g/8 oz plain flour
1 tsp baking powder
1/2 tsp bicarbonate of soda
75 g/3 oz golden caster sugar
1 medium egg
275 ml/9 fl oz milk
zest and 1 tbsp juice from
1 small orange
50 g/2 oz butter, melted
and cooled

Preheat the oven to 200°C/400°F/Gas Mark 6. Line a deep muffin tray with 10 deep paper muffin cases. Wet a sharp knife and chop the fruits into small chunks. Set them aside.

Sift the flour, baking powder and bicarbonate of soda into a large bowl. Add the sugar and make a well in the centre. In another bowl, beat the egg and milk together with the orange juice.

Add the milk to the bowl with the melted butter and the orange zest and beat with a fork until all the flour is combined but the mixture is still slightly lumpy. Fold in three-quarters of the chopped fruit and spoon into the paper cases. Sprinkle the remaining fruit over the top of each muffin.

Bake for about 20 minutes until risen, golden and firm. Cool on a wire rack and eat warm or cold. Keep for 24 hours sealed in an airtight container.

Blackcurrant Lemon Muffins

Makes 12

1 lemon
275 g/10 oz plain flour
1 tbsp baking powder
125 g/4 oz caster sugar
2 medium eggs
275 ml/9 fl oz milk
$1/2$ tsp vanilla extract
75 g/3 oz butter, melted
and cooled
150 g/5 oz fresh or frozen
blackcurrants, trimmed

Preheat the oven to 200°C/400°F/Gas Mark 6. Grease or line a deep 12-hole muffin tray with deep paper cases.

Finely grate the zest from the lemon into a bowl, then sift in the flour and baking powder and stir in the sugar. In another bowl, beat the eggs with the milk and vanilla extract.

Make a well in the centre and pour in the egg mixture and the cooled melted butter. Stir together with a fork until just combined and then gently fold in the blackcurrants.

Spoon into the muffin trays and bake for 20 minutes or until firm and golden. Leave in the tins for 4 minutes, then turn out onto a wire rack to finish cooling. Serve warm or cold. Best eaten on the day of baking.

Chunky Chocolate Muffins

Makes 12–14

To decorate:

75 g/3 oz granulated sugar
5 tbsp evaporated milk
125 g/4 oz dark
chocolate, chopped
40 g/1¹⁄₂ oz unsalted butter

To make the muffins:

125 g/4 oz soft margarine
125 g/4 oz golden caster sugar
2 medium eggs, beaten
25 g/1 oz cocoa powder
175 g/6 oz self-raising flour
1 tsp baking powder
2 tbsp milk
50 g/2 oz milk chocolate, chopped
50 g/2 oz dark or
white chocolate, chopped

Make the frosting first in order to allow it to cool. Place the sugar and evaporated milk in a heavy-based pan and stir over a low heat until every grain of sugar has dissolved. Simmer for 5 minutes but do not allow the mixture to boil. Remove from the heat, cool for 5 minutes, and then add the chocolate and butter. Stir until these melt. Pour the mixture into a bowl and chill for 2 hours until thickened.

Preheat the oven to 180˚C/350˚F/Gas Mark 4. Line one or two deep muffin trays with 12–14 paper cases, depending on the depth of the holes. Place the margarine and sugar in a bowl with the eggs and sift in the cocoa powder, flour and baking powder. Beat with the milk for about 2 minutes until smooth, then fold in the chopped chocolate.

Spoon into the paper cases and bake for 15–20 minutes until firm. Place on a wire rack to cool.

Remove the frosting from the fridge and beat to soften it slightly. Swirl it over the muffins. Keep in a cool place in a sealed container for 3–4 days.

Choc Chip Cherry Muffins

Makes 12

75 g/3 oz glacé cherries
75 g/3 oz milk or dark
chocolate chips
75 g/3 oz soft margarine
200 g/7 oz caster sugar
2 medium eggs
150 ml/¼ pint thickset
natural yogurt
5 tbsp milk
275 g/10 oz plain flour
1 tsp bicarbonate of soda

Preheat the oven to 200°C/400°F/Gas Mark 6. Line a deep 12-hole muffin tray with deep paper cases. Wash and dry the cherries. Chop them roughly, mix them with the chocolate chips and set aside.

Beat the margarine and sugar together, then whisk in the eggs, yogurt and milk. Sift in the flour and bicarbonate of soda. Stir until just combined.

Fold in three-quarters of the cherries and chocolate chips. Spoon the mixture into the cases, filling them two-thirds full. Sprinkle the remaining cherries and chocolate chips over the top.

Bake for about 20 minutes until golden and firm. Leave in the tins for 4 minutes, then turn out to cool on a wire rack. Serve straight away or keep for 24 hours in an airtight container.

Peaches & Cream Muffins

Makes 10

225 g/8 oz can peach slices or halves in syrup
125 g/4 oz self-raising flour
50 g/2 oz wholemeal self-raising flour
1/2 tsp cinnamon
175 g/6 oz butter, softened
175 g/6 oz golden caster sugar
3 medium eggs, beaten
1 tbsp golden syrup

To decorate:

2 tsp lemon juice
2 tbsp icing sugar
150 ml/1/4 pint whipping cream

Preheat the oven to 190°C/375°F/Gas Mark 5. Line a deep 12-hole muffin tray with 10 paper cases. Drain the peaches and chop 125 g/4 oz into small chunks.

Sift the flours and cinnamon into a bowl, adding any bran from the sieve, then add the butter, sugar and eggs. Beat for about 2 minutes, then fold in the golden syrup and chopped peaches.

Spoon the mixture into the paper cases and bake for about 20 minutes until well risen and springy in the centre. Remove to a wire rack to cool.

Place 50 g/2 oz sliced peaches in a blender or food processor with the lemon juice and icing sugar to make a purée (the rest of the can's weight is syrup). Whip the cream until it forms soft peaks and then fold in half the purée. Place a large spoonful of cream on top of each muffin, then swirl in a little extra purée. Refrigerate until needed and eat within 24 hours.

Choc Orange Marbled Muffins

Makes 10–12

175 g/6 oz soft margarine
175 g/6 oz caster sugar
3 medium eggs
175 g/6 oz self-raising flour
1 tsp baking powder
1 tbsp cocoa powder
finely grated zest and juice of
½ orange
4 tbsp clear honey, to glaze

Preheat the oven to 180°C/350°F/Gas Mark 4. Grease two deep 6-hole muffin trays, or line with 10–12 deep paper cases, depending on the depth of the holes.

Put the margarine, sugar, eggs, flour and baking powder into a large mixing bowl. Whisk the mixture together for about 2 minutes until smooth.

Place half the mixture into another bowl and sift over the cocoa, then stir in until blended. Stir the orange juice and zest into the other mixture.

Spoon the cocoa mixture evenly between the prepared tins. Spoon over the orange mixture and, using a flat-bladed knife, swirl through the two mixtures to make a marbled pattern.

Bake for 15–20 minutes until well risen and firm to the touch. Cool in the tins for 5 minutes, then turn out to cool on a wire rack. While still warm, drizzle each muffin with a little clear honey. Keep for 4 days in an airtight container.

Mini Chocolate Ripple Muffins

Makes 24

175 g/6 oz soft margarine
175 g/6 oz caster sugar
3 medium eggs
175 g/6 oz self-raising flour
1 tsp baking powder
1 tbsp cocoa powder
1 tbsp milk
1/2 tsp vanilla extract

Preheat the oven to 180°C/350°F/Gas Mark 4. Grease a 24-hole mini-muffin tray, or line with paper cases.

Put the margarine, sugar, eggs, flour and baking powder into a large mixing bowl. Whisk for about 2 minutes until smooth, then pour half the mixture into a separate bowl and sift the cocoa powder over it. Stir in the milk until blended. Stir the vanilla extract into the first mixture.

Spoon the cocoa mixture evenly between the prepared tins, then spoon over the vanilla mixture. Using a small spoon, swirl through the two mixtures to make a marbled pattern.

Bake for 12–15 minutes until well risen and firm to the touch. Cool in the tins for 5 minutes, then turn out to cool on a wire rack. Keep in an airtight container for 3–4 days.

Streusel-topped Banana Muffins

Makes 6

To decorate:

25 g/1 oz self-raising flour
15 g/¹/₂ oz butter
40 g/1¹/₂ oz demerara sugar
¹/₂ tsp ground cinnamon

To make the muffins:

125 g/4 oz self-raising
wholemeal flour
25 g/1 oz plain flour
2 medium ripe bananas,
about 175 g/6 oz
1 large egg
50 ml/2 fl oz sunflower oil
50 ml/2 fl oz milk

Preheat the oven to 200°C/400°F/Gas Mark 6. Line a deep muffin tray with 6 deep paper cases. Make the topping first by rubbing the butter into the flour until it resembles fine crumbs. Stir in the sugar and cinnamon and set aside.

To make the muffins, sift the flours into a bowl, then make a well in the centre. Mash the bananas with a fork and add them to the bowl.

In another bowl, beat the egg, oil and milk together and then add them to the bowl. Mix together until evenly blended, then spoon into the muffin cases, filling them two-thirds full.

Sprinkle the streusel topping over each muffin and bake for about 25 minutes until golden and a skewer inserted into the centre comes out clean. Eat fresh on the day of baking.

Pistachio Muffins

Makes 10

125 g/4 oz self-raising flour
125 g/4 oz butter, softened
125 g/4 oz golden
caster sugar
2 medium eggs, beaten
1 tbsp maple syrup or
golden syrup
50 g/2 oz pistachio nuts,
roughly chopped

To decorate:

225 g/8 oz golden icing sugar
125 g/4 oz unsalted
butter, softened
2 tsp lemon juice
25 g/1 oz pistachio
nuts, chopped

Preheat the oven to 200°C/400°F/Gas Mark 6. Line a deep 12-hole muffin tray with 10 deep paper cases.

Sift the flour into a bowl and add the butter, sugar and eggs. Beat for about 2 minutes, then fold in the syrup and chopped nuts.

Spoon the mixture into the paper cases and bake for about 20 minutes until well risen and springy in the centre. Remove to a wire rack to cool.

To decorate the cakes, sift the icing sugar into a bowl, then add the butter, lemon juice and 1 tablespoon hot water. Beat until light and fluffy, then swirl onto each cupcake with a small palette knife. Place the chopped pistachio nuts in a small shallow bowl. Dip the top of each muffin into the nuts to make an attractive topping. Keep for 4 days in an airtight container in a cool place.

Rhubarb Custard Muffins

Makes 12

225 g/8 oz pink rhubarb
25 g/1 oz vanilla custard powder
175 g/6 oz plain flour
2 tsp baking powder
125 g/4 oz golden caster sugar
100 ml/3^1/$_2$ fl oz milk
2 medium eggs, beaten
^{1}/$_2$ tsp vanilla extract
125 g/4 oz butter, melted
and cooled
golden caster sugar, for dusting

Preheat the oven to 180°C/350°F/Gas Mark 4. Oil or line a 12-hole deep muffin tray with deep muffin cases. Chop the rhubarb into pieces 1 cm/^{1}/$_2$ inch long.

Sift the custard powder, flour and baking powder into a bowl and stir in the sugar. In another bowl, beat the milk, eggs and vanilla extract together. Make a well in the centre of the dry ingredients and pour in the milk mixture.

Add the melted butter and beat together with a fork until just combined, then fold in the chopped rhubarb. Spoon the mixture into the cases and bake for 15–20 minutes until golden, risen and firm in the centre.

Leave in the tray to firm up for 5 minutes, then turn out onto a wire rack to cool. Serve warm, dusted with golden caster sugar. Eat on the day of baking.

Pineapple Carrot Muffins

Makes 12

175 g/6 oz self-raising
wholemeal flour
1 tsp baking powder
$^1/_2$ tsp ground cinnamon
pinch salt
150 ml/$^1/_4$ pint sunflower oil
150 g/5 oz soft light brown sugar
3 medium eggs, beaten
50 g/2 oz soft dried pineapple,
chopped
225 g/8 oz carrots, peeled and
finely grated

To decorate:

75 g/3 oz cream cheese
175 g/6 oz golden icing sugar
2 tsp lemon juice
50 g/2 oz soft dried pineapple
pieces, thinly sliced

Preheat the oven to 180°C/350°F/Gas Mark 4. Lightly oil a deep 12-hole muffin tray or line with deep paper cases.

Sift the flour, baking powder, cinnamon and salt into a bowl, including any bran from the sieve. Add the oil, sugar, eggs, chopped pineapple and grated carrots.

Beat until smooth, then spoon into the muffin cases. Bake for 20–25 minutes until risen and golden. Cool on a wire rack.

To decorate the muffins, beat the cream cheese and icing sugar together with the lemon juice to make a spreading consistency. Swirl the icing over the top of each cupcake, then top with a piece of dried pineapple. If chilled and sealed in an airtight container, these will keep for 3–4 days.

Very Berry Muffins

Makes 10

225 g/8 oz plain flour
1 tsp baking powder
$^{1}/_{2}$ tsp bicarbonate of soda
65 g/2$^{1}/_{2}$ oz golden caster sugar
1 medium egg
175 ml/6 fl oz milk
zest and 1 tbsp juice from
1 small orange
50 g/2 oz butter, melted
and cooled
125 g/4 oz fresh raspberries
50 g/ 2 oz dried cranberries

Preheat the oven to 200˚C/400˚F/Gas Mark 6. Line a deep 12-hole muffin tray with 10 deep paper cases.

Sift the flour, baking powder and bicarbonate of soda into a large bowl. Add the sugar and make a well in the centre. Beat the egg and milk together in a jug with the orange juice.

Pour the milk mixture into the bowl together with the cooled butter and the orange zest and beat lightly with a fork until all the flour is combined but the mixture is still slightly lumpy. Gently fold in the raspberries and cranberries and spoon into the paper cases.

Bake for about 20 minutes until firm and risen and a skewer inserted into the centre comes out clean. Cool on a wire rack. Eat warm or cold on the day of baking.

Spiced Apple Doughnuts

Makes 8

225 g/8 oz strong white flour
$^{1}/_{2}$ tsp salt
1$^{1}/_{2}$ tsp ground cinnamon
1 tsp easy-blend dried yeast
75 ml/3 fl oz warm milk
25 g/1 oz butter, melted
1 medium egg, beaten
oil, for deep-frying
4 tbsp caster sugar, to coat

For the filling

2 small eating apples, peeled,
cored and chopped
2 tsp soft light brown sugar
2 tsp lemon juice

Sift the flour, salt and 1 teaspoon of the cinnamon into a large bowl. Stir in the yeast and make a well in the centre. Add the milk, butter and egg and mix to a soft dough. Knead on a lightly floured surface for 10 minutes. Divide the dough into eight pieces and shape each into a ball. Put on a floured baking sheet, cover with oiled clingfilm and leave in a warm place for 1 hour, or until doubled in size.

To make the filling, put the apples in a saucepan with the sugar, lemon juice and 3 tablespoons water. Cover and simmer for about 10 minutes, then uncover and cook until fairly dry, stirring occasionally. Mash or blend to a purée in a food processor.

Pour enough oil into a deep-fat fryer or saucepan to come one-third of the way up the pan. Heat the oil to 180˚C/350˚F, then deep-fry the doughnuts for 1$^{1}/_{2}$–2 minutes on each side, until well browned.

Drain the doughnuts on absorbent kitchen paper, then roll in the caster sugar mixed with the remaining $^{1}/_{2}$ teaspoon ground cinnamon. Push a thick skewer into the centre to make a hole, then pipe in the apple filling. Serve warm or cold.

Chocolate Orange Rock Buns

Makes 12

200 g/7 oz self-raising flour
25 g/1 oz cocoa powder
1/2 tsp baking powder
125 g/4 oz butter
40 g/1 1/2 oz granulated sugar
50 g/2 oz candied
pineapple, chopped
50 g/2 oz ready-to-eat dried
apricots, chopped
50 g/2 oz glacé cherries, quartered
1 medium egg
finely grated zest
of 1/2 orange
1 tbsp orange juice
2 tbsp demerara sugar

Preheat the oven to 200°C/400°F/Gas Mark 6, 15 minutes before baking. Lightly oil two baking sheets, or line them with nonstick baking parchment. Sift the flour, cocoa powder and baking powder into a bowl. Cut the butter into small cubes. Add to the dry ingredients, then, using your hands, rub in until the mixture resembles fine breadcrumbs.

Add the granulated sugar, pineapple, apricots and cherries to the bowl and stir to mix. Lightly beat the egg together with the grated orange zest and juice. Drizzle the egg mixture over the dry ingredients and stir to combine. The mixture should be fairly stiff but not too dry; add a little more orange juice, if needed.

Using two teaspoons, shape the mixture into 12 rough heaps on the prepared baking sheets. Sprinkle generously with the demerara sugar. Bake in the preheated oven for 15 minutes, switching the baking sheets around after 10 minutes. Leave on the baking sheets for 5 minutes to cool slightly, then transfer to a wire rack to cool. Serve warm or cold.

Lemon Ginger Buns

Makes 15

175 g/6 oz butter or margarine
350 g/12 oz plain flour
2 tsp baking powder
¹/₂ tsp ground ginger
pinch salt
finely grated zest of 1 lemon
175 g/6 oz soft light brown sugar
125 g/4 oz sultanas
75 g/3 oz chopped mixed peel
25 g/1 oz stem ginger,
finely chopped
1 medium egg
juice of 1 lemon

Preheat the oven to 220°C/425°F/Gas Mark 7, 15 minutes before baking. Cut the butter or margarine into small pieces and place in a large bowl. Sift the flour, baking powder, ginger and salt together and add to the butter with the lemon zest.

Using the fingertips, rub the butter into the flour and spice mixture until it resembles coarse breadcrumbs. Stir in the sugar, sultanas, chopped mixed peel and stem ginger.

Add the egg and lemon juice to the mixture, then, using a round-bladed knife, stir well to mix. (The mixture should be quite stiff and just holding together.)

Place heaped tablespoons of the mixture onto a lightly oiled baking tray, making sure that the dollops of mixture are spaced well apart. Using a fork, rough up the edges of the buns and bake in the preheated oven for 12–15 minutes.

Leave the buns to cool for 5 minutes before transferring to a wire rack until cold, then serve. Otherwise, store the buns in an airtight container and eat within 3–5 days.

Jammy Buns

Makes 12

175 g/6 oz plain flour
175 g/6 oz wholemeal flour
2 tsp baking powder
150 g/5 oz butter or margarine
125 g/4 oz golden caster sugar
50 g/2 oz dried cranberries
1 large egg, beaten
1 tbsp milk
4–5 tbsp seedless raspberry jam

Preheat the oven to 190°C/375°F/Gas Mark 5, 10 minutes before baking. Lightly oil a large baking sheet.

Sift the flours and baking powder together into a large bowl, then tip in the grains remaining in the sieve.

Cut the butter or margarine into small pieces. It is easier to do this when the butter is in the flour, as it helps stop the butter from sticking to the knife.

Rub the butter into the flours until it resembles coarse breadcrumbs. Stir in the sugar and cranberries.

Using a round-bladed knife, stir in the beaten egg and milk. Mix to form a firm dough. Divide the mixture into 12 and roll into balls.

Place the dough balls on the baking tray, leaving enough space for expansion. Press your thumb into the centre of each ball to make a small hollow. Spoon a little of the jam into each hollow. Pinch lightly to seal the tops.

Bake in the preheated oven for 20–25 minutes until golden brown. Cool on a wire rack and serve.

Fruited Brioche Buns

Makes 12

225 g/8 oz strong white flour
pinch salt
1 tbsp caster sugar
10 g/¹/₄ oz sachet easy-blend
dried yeast
2 large eggs, beaten
50 g/2 oz butter, melted
beaten egg, to glaze

For the filling

40 g/1¹/₂ oz blanched
almonds, chopped
50 g/2 oz luxury mixed dried fruit
1 tsp light soft brown sugar
2 tsp orange liqueur or brandy

Preheat the oven to 220°C/425°F/Gas Mark 7, 15 minutes before baking. Sift the flour and salt into a bowl. Stir in the sugar and yeast. Make a well in the centre. Add the eggs, butter and 2 tablespoons warm water and mix to a soft dough. Knead the dough on a floured surface for 5 minutes until smooth and elastic. Put in an oiled bowl, cover with clingfilm and leave to rise for 1 hour, or until it has doubled in size. Mix the filling ingredients together, cover the bowl and leave to soak while the dough is rising. Re-knead the dough for a minute or two, then divide into 12 pieces.

Take one piece at a time and flatten three quarters into a 6.5 cm/ 2¹/₂ inch round. Spoon the filling into the centre; pinch the edges together to enclose. Put seam-side down into a well-greased, fluted, 12-hole bun tray.

Shape the smaller piece of dough into a round and place on top of the larger one. Push a finger or floured wooden spoon handle through the middle of the top one and into the bottom one to join them together. Repeat with the remaining balls of dough. Cover the brioches with oiled clingfilm and leave for about 20 minutes until well risen. Brush the brioches with beaten egg and bake in the oven for 10–12 minutes until golden. Cool on a wire rack and serve.

Hot Cross Buns

Makes 12

500 g/1 lb 2 oz strong white
bread flour
1 tsp salt
2 tsp mixed spice
50 g/2 oz soft light brown sugar
7 g sachet fast-action dried yeast
275 ml/9 fl oz milk
1 medium egg, beaten
50 g/2 oz butter, melted
and cooled
225 g/8 oz mixed dried fruit

For the decoration:

1 medium egg, beaten
75 g/3 oz shortcrust pastry
50 g/2 oz caster sugar

Sift the flour, salt and spice into a bowl and then stir in the sugar and yeast. In a jug, whisk together the milk and the egg. Add the liquid to the flour in the bowl with the cooled melted butter and mix to a soft dough. Knead for 10 minutes by hand, or for 5 minutes using a tabletop mixer fitted with a dough hook, until smooth and elastic.

Knead in the fruit and then place the dough in a bowl. Cover it with oiled clingfilm. Leave in a warm place for about 1 hour until doubled in size. Butter a large 32 x 23 cm/12 x 9 inch baking tray or a roasting tin. Cut the dough into 12 chunks and roll each one into a ball. Place in the tray, leaving enough space for the buns to rise and spread out. Cover with the oiled clingfilm and leave for about 45 minutes until doubled in size.

Preheat the oven to 200°C/400°F/Gas Mark 6. Discard the clingfilm and brush the buns with the beaten egg. Roll the pastry into long thin strips. Place pastry strips crossways on each bun to make crosses. Repeat on all the buns. Bake for 20–25 minutes until risen and golden.

Heat 2 tablespoons of water and add the caster sugar, continuing to heat gently until the sugar is completely dissolved. While still hot, turn the buns out of the tray and place on a wire rack. Brush the sugar glaze over the warm buns and leave to cool. These are best eaten on the day of baking. Split and toast any leftovers and serve with butter.

Chocolate Chelsea Buns

Makes 12

75 g/3 oz dried pears,
finely chopped
1 tbsp apple or orange juice
225 g/8 oz strong plain flour
1 tsp ground cinnamon
1¹/₂ tsp salt
40 g/1¹/₂ oz butter
11/2 tsp easy-blend dried yeast
125 ml/4 fl oz warm milk
1 medium egg, lightly beaten
75 g/3 oz dark chocolate, chopped
3 tbsp maple syrup

Preheat the oven to 190°C/ 375°F/Gas Mark 5, 10 minutes before baking. Lightly oil an 18 cm/7 inch square tin. Place the pears in a bowl with the fruit juice, stir then cover and leave to soak while making the dough. Sift the flour, cinnamon and salt into a bowl, rub in 25 g/1 oz of the butter then stir in the yeast and make a well in the middle. Add the milk and egg and mix to a soft dough. Knead on a floured surface for 10 minutes, until smooth and elastic, then place in a bowl. Cover with clingfilm and leave in a warm place to rise for 1 hour or until doubled in size.

Turn out on a lightly floured surface and knead the dough lightly before rolling out to a rectangle, about 30.5 x 23 cm/12 x 9 inches. Melt the remaining butter and brush over. Spoon the pears and chocolate evenly over the dough leaving a 2.5 cm/ 1 inch border, then roll up tightly, starting at a long edge. Cut into 12 equal slices, then place, cut-side up in the tin. Cover and leave to rise for 25 minutes, or until doubled in size.

Bake on the centre shelf for 30 minutes, or until well risen and golden brown. Cover with kitchen foil after 20 minutes, if the filling is starting to brown too much. Brush with the maple syrup while hot, then leave in the tin for 10 minutes to cool slightly. Turn out onto a rack and leave to cool. Separate the buns and serve warm.

Traditional Oven Scones

Makes 8

225 g/8 oz self-raising flour
1 tsp baking powder
pinch salt
40 g/1¹/₂ oz butter, cubed
15 g/¹/₂oz caster sugar
150 ml/¹/₄ pint milk, plus
1 tbsp for brushing
1 tbsp plain flour, to dust

For a lemon and sultana scone variation

50 g/2 oz sultanas
finely grated rind of ¹/₂ lemon
beaten egg, to glaze

Preheat the oven to 220°C/425°F/Gas Mark 7, 15 minutes before baking. Sift the flour, baking powder and salt into a large bowl. Rub in the butter until the mixture resembles fine breadcrumbs. Stir in the sugar and mix in enough milk to give a fairly soft dough.

Knead the dough on a lightly floured surface for a few seconds until smooth. Roll out until 2.5 cm/1 inch thick and stamp out 6.5 cm/2¹/₂ inch rounds with a floured plain cutter.

Place on an oiled baking sheet and brush the tops with milk (do not brush it over the sides or the scones will not rise properly). Dust with a little plain flour.

Bake in the preheated oven for 12–15 minutes, or until well risen and golden brown. Transfer to a wire rack and serve warm or leave to cool completely. (The scones are best eaten on the day of baking but may be kept in an airtight tin for up to 2 days.)

For lemon and sultana scones, stir in the sultanas and lemon rind with the sugar. Roll out until 2 cm/³/₄ inches thick and cut into 8 fingers, 10 x 2.5 cm/4 x 1 inch in size. Bake the scones as before.

Easy Danish Pastries

Makes 16

500 g/1 lb 2 oz strong white flour
1/2 tsp salt
350 g/12 oz butter
7 g sachet fast-action yeast
50 g/2 oz caster sugar
150 ml/1/4 pint lukewarm milk
2 medium eggs, beaten

For the filling and topping:

225 g/8 oz ready-made almond paste or
marzipan, grated
8 canned apricot halves, drained
1 egg, beaten
125 g/4 oz fondant icing sugar
50 g/2 oz glacé cherries
50 g/2 oz flaked almonds

Sift the flour and salt into a bowl, add 50 g/2 oz of the butter and rub in until it resembles fine crumbs. Stir in the yeast and sugar. Stir in the milk and eggs and mix to a soft dough. Knead by hand for 10 minutes until smooth or for 5 minutes in a tabletop mixer fitted with a dough hook. Cover with oiled clingfilm and leave for about 1 hour in a warm place or until doubled in size. Place on a floured surface and knead for about 4 minutes until smooth. Roll out to 20 x 35 cm/8 x 14 inches. Dot two thirds with half the remaining butter. Fold the plain third up over the buttered section, then fold the top third over this to form a square parcel. Press the edges to seal, then turn, with the fold to the left. Roll out again to a rectangle and dot with the remaining butter. Chill for 15 minutes, then roll out and fold again. Roll, fold and chill once more.

Preheat the oven to 220°C/425°F/Gas Mark 7. Roll out the dough to 55 cm/ 22 inches and cut into 16 squares. Put 25 g/1 oz of the almond paste or marzipan in the centre of each. Cut the corners almost to the middle on eight of the squares and fold over the alternate points. Top each of the remaining squares with an apricot half and fold the opposite corners over. Arrange on buttered baking sheets and leave to rise for 20 minutes until puffy. Brush with egg and bake for 15 minutes until golden. When cold, mix the fondant icing sugar with enough water to make a smooth icing. Drizzle over the pastries and place a halved cherry on the windmill shapes. Scatter the others with flaked almonds and leave to set for 30 minutes.

Luxury Mince Pies

Makes 20

275 g/10 oz plain flour
25 g/1 oz ground almonds
175 g/6 oz butter, diced
75 g/3 oz icing sugar
zest of 1 lemon, finely grated
1 egg yolk
3 tbsp milk

For the filling:

225 g/8 oz mincemeat
1 tbsp dark rum or orange juice
zest of 1 orange, finely grated
75 g/3 oz dried cranberries
icing sugar, for dusting

Sift the flour and ground almonds into a bowl or a food processor and add the butter. Rub in, or process, until the mixture resembles fine crumbs. Sift in the icing sugar and stir in the lemon zest. Whisk the egg yolk and milk together in a separate bowl and stir into the mixture until a soft dough forms. Wrap the pastry in clingfilm and chill for 30 minutes.

Preheat the oven to 200°C/400°F/Gas Mark 6. Grease two 12-hole patty tins. Roll out the pastry on a lightly floured surface to 3 mm/ 1/8 inch thickness. Cut out 20 rounds using a 7.5 cm/3 inch fluted round pastry cutter. Re-roll the trimmings into thin strips.

Mix the filling ingredients together in a bowl. Place 1 tablespoon of the filling in each pastry case, then dampen the edges of each case with a little water. Put four strips of pastry over the top of each case to form a lattice.

Bake for 10–15 minutes until the pastry is crisp. Dust with icing sugar and serve hot or cold.

Mini Strawberry Tartlets

Makes 12 tartlets

225 g/8 oz plain flour
25 g/1 oz icing sugar
125 g/4 oz butter, diced
25 g/1 oz ground almonds
1 egg yolk

For the filling:

85 ml/3 fl oz double cream
175 g/6 oz full-fat cream cheese
25 g/1 oz vanilla caster sugar
2 tbsp amaretto almond-flavoured
liqueur
250 g/9 oz strawberries, hulled,
and halved if large
2 tbsp sieved raspberry jam
small mint leaves,
to decorate

Sift the flour and icing sugar into a bowl and add the diced butter. Rub the butter into the flour with your fingertips until the mixture resembles fine crumbs. Alternatively, place the flour, icing sugar and butter in a food processor and process until fine crumbs form. Stir in the ground almonds and egg yolk and mix with 1 tablespoon cold water to form a soft dough. Cover with clingfilm and chill for 30 minutes.

Preheat the oven to 200°C/400°F/Gas Mark 6 and grease a 12-hole muffin tin. Roll out the dough on a lightly floured surface to 6 mm/ 1/4 inch thickness and cut out twelve 10 cm/4 inch circles. Press the circles into the holes in the tin, loosely fluting up the edges. Prick the bases with a fork and bake for 12–15 minutes until light golden. Leave to cool in the tins for 3 minutes, then remove to cool completely on a wire rack.

To make the filling, whip the cream until stiff then mix with the cream cheese, sugar and liqueur. Chill until needed and then spoon into the pastry cases.

Arrange the fresh strawberries on top and brush lightly with a little jam to glaze. Decorate with small fresh mint leaves and serve immediately.

Index

Index